THE ATHLETE'S NIL PLAYBOOK

THE ATHLETE'S NIL PLAYBOOK

The Complete Guide to Owning and Profiting from Your **Name, Image,** and **Likeness**

KRISTI DOSH

FOREWORD by HALEY and HANNA CAVINDER

WILEY

Copyright © 2025 by John Wiley & Sons. All rights reserved, including rights for text and data mining and training of artificial intelligence technologies or similar technologies.

Published by John Wiley & Sons, Inc., Hoboken, New Jersey.
Published simultaneously in Canada.

No part of this publication may be reproduced, stored in a retrieval system, or transmitted in any form or by any means, electronic, mechanical, photocopying, recording, scanning, or otherwise, except as permitted under Section 107 or 108 of the 1976 United States Copyright Act, without either the prior written permission of the Publisher, or authorization through payment of the appropriate per-copy fee to the Copyright Clearance Center, Inc., 222 Rosewood Drive, Danvers, MA 01923, (978) 750-8400, fax (978) 750-4470, or on the web at www.copyright.com. Requests to the Publisher for permission should be addressed to the Permissions Department, John Wiley & Sons, Inc., 111 River Street, Hoboken, NJ 07030, (201) 748-6011, fax (201) 748-6008, or online at http://www.wiley.com/go/permission.

The manufacturer's authorized representative according to the EU General Product Safety Regulation is Wiley-VCH GmbH, Boschstr. 12, 69469 Weinheim, Germany, e-mail: Product_Safety@wiley.com.

Trademarks: Wiley and the Wiley logo are trademarks or registered trademarks of John Wiley & Sons, Inc. and/or its affiliates in the United States and other countries and may not be used without written permission. All other trademarks are the property of their respective owners. John Wiley & Sons, Inc. is not associated with any product or vendor mentioned in this book.

Limit of Liability/Disclaimer of Warranty: While the publisher and author have used their best efforts in preparing this book, they make no representations or warranties with respect to the accuracy or completeness of the contents of this book and specifically disclaim any implied warranties of merchantability or fitness for a particular purpose. No warranty may be created or extended by sales representatives or written sales materials. The advice and strategies contained herein may not be suitable for your situation. You should consult with a professional where appropriate. Further, readers should be aware that websites listed in this work may have changed or disappeared between when this work was written and when it is read. Neither the publisher nor authors shall be liable for any loss of profit or any other commercial damages, including but not limited to special, incidental, consequential, or other damages.

For general information on our other products and services or for technical support, please contact our Customer Care Department within the United States at (800) 762-2974, outside the United States at (317) 572-3993 or fax (317) 572-4002.

Wiley also publishes its books in a variety of electronic formats. Some content that appears in print may not be available in electronic formats. For more information about Wiley products, visit our web site at www.wiley.com.

Library of Congress Cataloging-in-Publication Data is Available:

ISBN 9781394354054 (paper)
ISBN 9781394354061 (ePub)
ISBN 9781394354078 (ePDF)

Cover Design: Wiley
Cover Images: © Mysterylab/stock.adobe.com, © Tartila/stock.adobe.com
Author photo: © Kristi Dosh

Disclaimer: The material in this book is made available for educational purposes. It provides general information and is not intended to provide specific legal advice. This information should not be used as a substitute for competent legal advice from a licensed attorney in your jurisdiction.

SKY10105509_051425

To every athlete who contributed to this book or shared their NIL journey with me over the past four years, thank you! It's been the highlight of my career watching you all take advantage of these new opportunities, and I can't wait to see what you do next.

Contents

Foreword	*xiii*
Introduction	*xv*

1 NIL Rules in College and High School Sports   **1**

How We Got Here	3
NCAA NIL Rules	8
The Evolution of the NCAA's NIL Rules	9
NAIA Rules	14
NJCAA Rules	15
Institutional Rules	15
High School Rules	17
Youth Athletes	18
International Athletes	21
Types of Visas	22
Limitations on NIL for International Athletes	32
Weighing the Risks	36
What's Next for International Athletes	37

2 NIL Activities and Opportunities   **39**

Social Media Marketing	40
Important: FTC Requirements	43
Affiliate and Ambassador Roles	44

Lessons, Camps, and Clinics	47
Solo Planning Checklist	49
Appearances and Autographs	52
Merchandise and Memorabilia	54
Group Licensing and Team-Wide Deals	57
NFTs	58
Podcasts, Radio, and Blogs	58
Books	61
Public Speaking and Messaging	65
Music	69
Art	69
Car Deals and Other Free Products and Services	72
Car Deals	72
Medical Services	73
Real Estate Training	74
3 Defining and Growing Your Personal Brand	**77**
Developing Your NIL Strategy: The Three Questions	77
What Do You Already Enjoy Doing Outside of Your Sport?	78
What Do You Want to Do After Graduation?	79
What Are One to Three Things You Want to Be Known For?	80
The Riches Are in the Niches	84
4 Social Media Marketing	**89**
Optimizing Your Profile	90
Choosing the Right Username	90
Choosing the Right Profile Photo	91
Writing the Perfect Bio	92

How to Grow Your Following and Engagement 94

Being Strategic About Your Social Content 95

Utilizing Content Franchises 98

Building a Community for Long-Term Success 100

Choosing Your Social Channels 101

Post Ideas for Athletes 102

Getting Verified on Instagram 104

5 Finding Deals, Pitching Yourself, Pricing, and Negotiations 107

Where to Find Deals 107

Marketplaces 108

Collectives 111

Proactive Outreach 112

The How and Who 114

The Pitch 116

Email Pitch Template 120

Pitching by DM 122

How Most Deals Work 123

Negotiating the Deal 123

Pricing 124

Social Media Content Creator Pricing Guide 127

6 Working with Third Parties: Collectives, Marketing Agencies, and More 133

Collectives 133

What Is an NIL Collective? 133

Working with an NIL Collective 136

What to Know Before Signing a Collective Contract 141

Marketing Agencies 146

Third Parties Offering Advances 147

7 Licensing and Intellectual Property 151

Protecting Your IP Without Violating Someone Else's 152

Group Licensing and Co-Branding 154

What to Know Before Opting into Group Licensing Agreements 155

Jerseys and Shirzees 158

T-Shirts and Other Apparel 159

Trading Cards 161

Video Games 162

Other Group Licensing Opportunities 163

Trademarks 165

8 NIL Agents 171

Who Needs an Agent? 172

Questions to Ask Before Signing with an Agent 173

Things to Look for in Your Agency Contract Before You Sign 177

Term 177

Commission 178

Scope of Representation 179

Termination 179

Disputes 180

What It's Like to Work with an Agent 181

Having the Wrong Agent Is Worse Than Having No Agent 182

Parents, Family Members, and Friends as Agents 186

9 Contracts and Other Legal Issues 191

Benefits of a Written Contract 192

Understand Expectations 192

Preserve Your Ownership Rights 192

Get Paid – and on Time 192

Avoid Conflict ... 193
Act Like a Professional ... 193
Understanding Contracts for Content Creators ... 193
Unfavorable Compensation and Payment Terms ... 194
Excessive Licensing and Usage Rights ... 194
Agreeing to Be Exclusive ... 195
Right of First Refusal ... 197
Ambiguous Deliverables and Expectations ... 198
Edits ... 199
Unreasonable Termination Clauses ... 199
Use of School Logos, Colors, or Facilities ... 200
Indemnification and Liability ... 200
One-Sided Contract Terms or Negotiations ... 201

10 Growing and Maintaining Your Brand Beyond College ... **205**
Continuing to Work with Brands After Graduation ... 206
Content Strategy ... 208
Building Lasting Relationships ... 211
Making Connections ... 212

11 The Future of NIL and Revenue Sharing in College Sports ... **215**
The Future of NIL ... 215
Increased Institutional Involvement ... 216
Revenue Sharing ... 216
Back Pay Provisions ... 217
Revenue Sharing Model ... 220
Roster and Scholarship Changes ... 221
New Financial Aid and Revenue Sharing Agreements ... 224
Ongoing Legal Challenges ... 228

Conclusion	231
Acknowledgments	233
About the Author	235
Notes	237
Index	247

Foreword

When we first heard about NIL (Name, Image, Likeness), it felt like a game-changer – literally. For us, it wasn't just about sponsorships and deals; it was about taking control of our story, our brand, and our future. As athletes, we're used to the hustle on the court, but NIL taught us how to hustle off the court, too, turning our passion into opportunities that go beyond the game.

Our journey in NIL has been filled with lessons. We learned how to navigate partnerships, negotiate deals, and balance the demands of being both athletes and entrepreneurs. It wasn't always easy. There were moments of doubt, times when we wondered if we were doing it right. But with the right guidance and a strong support system, we found our rhythm – just like we do when we're in sync on the court. Having the right people in our corner made all the difference. Our agents, Jeff Hoffman and Alexi Hecht, have been instrumental in guiding us through the complexities of NIL, ensuring we not only secured the right opportunities but also stayed true to our values and vision.

The Athlete's NIL Playbook is the guide we wish we had when we started. It's more than just strategies and rules; it's a roadmap to building your personal brand with authenticity and purpose. This book breaks down complex concepts into actionable steps, helping athletes of all levels understand how to maximize their NIL potential while staying true to who they are.

What we love most about NIL is that it's not one-size-fits-all. Whether you're a student-athlete at a big program or a hidden gem at a smaller school, there are opportunities out there waiting for you. NIL isn't just for the stars; it's for anyone willing to put in the work, be creative, and tell their story.

As you dive into this playbook, remember this: Your brand is powerful because it's yours. No one can tell your story the way you can. Use your voice, lean into your passions, and don't be afraid to bet on yourself. NIL has given athletes a platform like never before – what you do with it is up to you.

– Haley and Hanna Cavinder

Introduction

One of the first topics I covered when I started writing about the business of college sports was Ed O'Bannon's lawsuit, which centered around the use of the likeness of college athletes in EA Sports video games without providing compensation to the athletes. Although the judge ruled in favor of O'Bannon, her decision didn't usher in name, image, and likeness (NIL) rights but instead cost-of-attendance stipends.

At the time, athletes in all of the major organizations that govern college athletics – the NAIA, NCAA, and NJCAA – prohibited athletes from earning money from activities that used their name, image, or likeness. This meant they couldn't get paid to promote a brand on their social media, to sign an autograph, or to have their name on a jersey. Or, in the case of O'Bannon, for being depicted in a video game.

In the decade since the case was decided in 2014, I've covered multiple lawsuits and rules changes that have increasingly provided new benefits to college athletes. It wasn't until 2021, however, that college athletes were finally able to profit off their name, image, and likeness without fear of losing their eligibility. Since then, NIL rights have trickled down to many high school and youth athletes.

Much of the conversation in the media is consumed with the large sums of money being offered to top recruits and current athletes, in sports like football and men's basketball. There are also numerous athletes who've become household names thanks to their large social media followings that have allowed them to sign lucrative marketing deals, such as LSU gymnast Livvy Dunne and women's basketball athletes Haley and Hanna Cavinder.

I've interviewed and interacted with thousands of college athletes since the NIL rules were changed in 2021 through both my reporting and speaking on campuses. There are incredible untold stories of athletes across every sport who've been able to pay tuition and rent, buy reliable transportation, and save for their future thanks to NIL. Some have even set themselves up for success beyond graduation by gaining skills from NIL that make them more marketable in their career field, introduce them to valuable contacts, or even enable them to start their own businesses that aren't dependent on their athletic participation.

Certainly it's true that NIL has introduced new realities in recruiting, transferring, and the relationship between donors and athletes. However, if we put that aside for a moment, it's worth noting that it has also allowed athletes to earn revenue from writing books, performing music, creating apparel and other merchandise, coaching youth athletes, and more.

Over the past 15 years, I've spoken on dozens of campuses about preparing for life after sport. One of the top complaints I heard from athletes was that they didn't have time to do internships like their non-athlete teammates and didn't know what to put on their resumes as they entered the workforce. NIL has offered opportunities to add hard skills to the soft skills they gain as athletes, including video production and editing, social media marketing, instruction, and more. I've even met athletes who've asked for micro-internships with companies as part of their NIL deals in order to get experience in their chosen field or for calls with the CEO to make valuable connections.

Leah Clapper, a former UF gymnast who served as a teaching assistant in my NIL course, was able to generate revenue not only from her own social following but also from creating user-generated content (UGC) for brands. This work followed her after graduation, and she was recruited by a venture capital company to run their social media and produce their podcast thanks in no small part to the video skills she honed while working on her own NIL deals.

Anna Camden, a women's basketball athlete at Penn State and then Richmond, had aspirations of being a sports broadcaster one day. It's a dream she's quickly making a reality as she completes her time as a college athlete.

As part of Meta's Empower program – where she was chosen from hundreds of applicants to take part in a small-group NIL program – she connected with agent Pat Curran. She mentioned to him that she wanted to be a sports broadcaster, and he suggested she start using her social media platform to create content analyzing sports so she could start building a portfolio and maybe even attract attention from someone in the industry.

It only took two weeks for her new plan to land her an incredible opportunity. Camden saw Pat give advice to his social media followers about stitching content with Richard Jefferson, a basketball analyst for ESPN. So she created a stitch, and two days later she was making her ESPN debut on *NBA Today*. Since then, she's had additional opportunities to work with CBS and the Big Ten Network during the Big Ten's men's basketball tournament in 2023, as a sports anchor on the Centre County Report, a student-run newscast at Penn State, and as a sideline reporter for the University of Richmond.

These are two quick examples of athletes who've leveraged NIL opportunities to create meaningful change in their lives that extends beyond their collegiate athlete experience. It's my favorite part of NIL, and I can't wait to share even more athlete stories with you within the pages of this book.

Although I will include stories about some of the most well-known college athletes in order to give a full 10,000-foot view of the NIL marketplace, I've attempted to include stories, advice, and tips that can help *any* athlete leverage their NIL, regardless of their level, school, or sport.

xvii

Introduction

This book isn't just for athletes, though; it's also a practical primer for anyone looking to get involved in this burgeoning industry. New jobs have been created on campuses and within a variety of companies working in this space to support athletes and institutions.

For the athletes reading this – or the parents who will distill it down for them later – I hope you find these stories inspiring and that the practical how-to advice allows you to create your own opportunities. NIL is for everyone, and I can't wait for you to be the next athlete story I'm telling!

Chapter 1

NIL Rules in College and High School Sports

What Is NIL?

NIL stands for "name, image, and likeness." In the context of college sports, it's used to identify opportunities for athletes to earn money through activities they engage in, or products they create, that rely on their name, image, or likeness. Examples include content creation for brands on social media, signing autographs, teaching lessons, coaching at a camp, creating their own products like T-shirts, and earning from trading cards, jerseys, and other merchandise. We'll dive into more ways athletes can monetize their NIL in Chapter 2.

In October 2020, NAIA athlete Chloe Mitchell became the first college athlete to legally monetize her name, image, and likeness. As an incoming freshman at Aquinas College in Grand Rapids, Michigan, Mitchell was able to quickly leverage her NIL following the rules change to work with brands based on her massive social following, which she'd grown from just 32 followers to more than two million during the COVID-19 pandemic as she turned a backyard shed into her own personal retreat, documenting it all for TikTok along the way.

The NCAA and NJCAA followed suit and began allowing their athletes to monetize their NIL in July 2021. Since then, college athletes at every level, in every division, in every sport at every school have engaged in NIL activities. Naysayers who doubted that athletes beyond the most visible sports – football and men's basketball – could monetize their NIL have been proved wrong. Both male and female athletes across the college landscape have received cash, free products, meals, and more in exchange for social media posts, personal appearances, and other uses of their NIL.

Organizations Governing Intercollegiate Athletics

- National Collegiate Athletic Association (NCAA)
  - Divided into: Division I (DI), Division II (DII), and Division III (DIII)
    - Division I football is divided into: Football Bowl Subdivision (FBS) and Football Championship Subdivision (FCS)
      - Note: Within the FBS, you'll hear the terms *Power 5/4* and the *Group of 5*. The Power 5 comprises these conferences: Atlantic Coast Conference (ACC), Big 12, Big Ten, Pac-12, and Southeastern Conference (SEC). The Power 4 removes the Pac-12 because it was down to only two schools in 2024. The Group of 5 comprises these conferences: American Athletic Conference (The American), Conference USA (CUSA), Mid-American Conference, Mountain West Conference, and Sun Belt Conference.
- National Association of Intercollegiate Athletics (NAIA)
- National Junior College Athletic Association (NJCAA)

NIL hasn't been limited to college athletes, either. Since rule changes in the NAIA, NCAA, and NJCAA in 2020 and 2021, state laws and state high school sports association rules have been passed and amended to allow high school athletes in more than half the states to participate in NIL deals as well. Major national brands like Nike, Kay Jewelers, and Panini have expanded their marketing efforts to work with high school athletes.

Unfortunately, there's a patchwork of state laws and institutional/organizational rules across the country that mean one college or high school athlete might have to abide by different rules than another. Let's take a look at how we got here, and the key rules you need to know at each level to ensure you remain eligible.

> Note: If you're not as interested in the history of the movement toward granting athletes NIL rights, skip this next section and go straight to the rules to ensure you're engaging in NIL safely.

How We Got Here

Prior to the NIL rules changing in 2020 (NAIA) and 2021 (NCAA), athletes were prohibited from making money from their name, image, or likeness. This prevented athletes from being compensated for social media posts featuring brands, getting paid to speak, selling their own merchandise, or anything else that relied on their NIL.

It is important to note the NCAA had a waiver process through which athletes could get approval for ventures that didn't involve their athletic ability or notoriety as an athlete. A source from the NCAA told me in 2019 that over the previous five years it had approved approximately 90% of requests received, totaling nearly 400.

For example, Arike Ogunbowale received a waiver from the NCAA in 2018 to compete on *Dancing with the Stars*, which allowed her to keep any money earned from the show. However, she wasn't allowed to promote her appearance, which included having to skip a group appearance with other dancers on *Good Morning America*.

However, other athletes had a more difficult time getting waivers. UCF kicker Donald Da La Haye was ruled ineligible after he refused conditions the NCAA put on his successful YouTube channel, namely that he had to have a nonmonetized channel that didn't take advantage of YouTube's ad network.[1]

Shortly thereafter, Texas A&M freshman track and field athlete Ryan Trahan was also temporarily ruled ineligible for a similar issue with his YouTube channel. The problem? It featured both his running and a water bottle company he created in high school. He was later granted a waiver but required to keep separate social media channels for his running and his business.[2]

Jeremy Bloom is one of the more famous cases of an athlete who was ruled ineligible thanks to his promotional work. Bloom was an Olympic and World Cup skier who had endorsed ski equipment, modeled, and taken advantage of other opportunities prior to college enrollment. Then he was recruited to by the University of Colorado to play football.

At the time, athletes could compete collegiately in one sport and play another professionally, with the caveat that they couldn't receive income for endorsing products for the other sport (although they could collect salaries or signing bonuses, such as the $1.75 million bonus Roscoe Crosby received from the Kansas City Royals while still playing football for Clemson).

Colorado's initial efforts to obtain a waiver so Bloom could play were initially denied. As a result, Bloom discontinued his skiing endorsements and other unauthorized activity. Although he was able to then play football at Colorado, he later sued the NCAA over its rules.

After giving up his endorsements for two seasons at Colorado, Bloom needed them to help fund his training for the Olympics

The Athlete's NIL Playbook

coming up in 2006 in Torino, Italy. When the NCAA wouldn't allow it, he took them to court. Ultimately, he lost at the trial court level and again when he appealed. It ended his collegiate football career, although he did go on to compete in two more Olympics and played in the NFL for one season.[3]

The rule changes in July 2021 would change all of that for athletes moving forward. The question of how and why the changes happened is more a game of dominos than a clear-cut answer as a result of just one event.

It can be argued that Sam Keller and Ed O'Bannon's lawsuits against the NCAA, Collegiate Licensing Company (CLC), and Electronic Arts, each filed in 2009, caused the first domino to fall. Both cases argued that athletes should be compensated for use of their name, image, and likeness in EA Sports's video games.

O'Bannon brought his case after seeing himself in EA Sports's *NCAA Basketball 09* game. Although the player was unnamed, he wore a UCLA jersey, played O'Bannon's power forward position, shot left-handed, wore his No. 31 jersey, and matched his height, weight, and skin tone.

Sam Keller, a former Nebraska football athlete, filed a similar suit shortly before O'Bannon, also challenging the use of athlete NIL in EA Sports video games. However, the cases differed slightly in that Keller only sought payment to college athletes who'd already been included in the EA Sports games, while O'Bannon was asking additionally for an injunction that would prohibit the games from being produced until athletes could be paid for the use of their NIL.[4]

Electronic Arts and CLC settled their parts of the video game claims for $40 million, which was paid out to approximately 100,000 then-current and former athletes who had appeared in the *NCAA Basketball, March Madness,* and *NCAA Football* games since 2003. The NCAA settled its part of the Keller suit for $20 million, but the O'Bannon case proceeded to trial in 2014.

Ultimately, Judge Claudia Wilken ruled the NCAA's practice of barring payments to athletes violated antitrust laws. However, instead of ushering in full NIL rights at that time, she allowed schools to begin offering full cost-of-attendance scholarships, which allowed for more compensation than the previous tuition and room-and-board scholarships.

Also in 2014, the Division I Council approved allowing athletic departments to provide unlimited meals to athletes after UConn men's basketball athlete Shabazz Napier told reporters at the NCAA Tournament that he sometimes went to bed starving because he couldn't afford food.

Following O'Bannon, additional class-action lawsuits were filed by student-athletes attacking the NCAA's rules that restricted payments and other benefits to athletes. The most important would be multiple cases filed in 2014 and 2015 that were consolidated into the *NCAA v. Alston* case before the United States Supreme Court in 2021.

Some narratives wrongly say that the *Altson* case caused the change in NIL rules because of comments some of the justices wrote in the opinion. Although the case certainly impacted how the NCAA decided to handle the rule change, the case itself didn't rule on NIL specifically. Instead, it removed any limitations on "education-related benefits." The change allowed for universities to provide noncash education-related benefits such as computers, science equipment, music instruments, and more. It also allowed for the payment of study abroad and tutoring expenses, post-eligibility scholarships, post-eligibility internships, and more.

The end result was the allowance of awards up to $5,980 per athlete per year for education-related expenses, dubbed "Alston awards." Each school distributes these according to their own policies and budgets, but most make them dependent on certain academic progress. Alston awards are also expected to undergo some changes – including elimination – at many institutions as revenue sharing is implemented under the *House* settlement (discussed in Chapter 11).

The main impetus for the NIL rule changes, however, was the passage of multiple state laws that allowed college athletes to begin being paid for their NIL. The first of these was passed in California in September 2019, the Fair Pay to Play Act. It was initially set to take effect in 2023, which would presumably give the NCAA time to change its rules and for schools to prepare for the new reality.

However, other states quickly began to consider similar rules and setting earlier implementation dates. Colorado passed its NIL law in March 2020 with an effective date of January 1, 2023. Then in June 2020, Florida passed its own NIL law that moved the date up to July 1, 2021.

By July 1, 2021, more than two dozen states had passed NIL laws. Although they all had a similar intent, there were plenty of differences. Some specifically prohibited certain categories of NIL deals, such as alcohol, tobacco, adult entertainment, prescription drugs, and more. Mississippi was the first state to ban high school athletes in its law that allowed NIL for college athletes, followed later by Texas and Illinois.

The NCAA had been set to pass a set of NIL rules with what it called "guardrails." For example, there were limitations on engaging in deals that conflicted with existing institutional sponsorships or using institutional facilities in the course of their NIL activities. There was also a disclosure requirement that required athletes to disclose NIL deals to a third-party administrator in advance.

However, as the NCAA was preparing to vote on the new rules at its January 2021 convention, it received a letter from the Justice Department expressing concerns about the rules and whether they complied with antitrust laws.[5] This caused the association to delay voting on the NIL rules.

NIL Rules in College and High School Sports

As the clock ticked down to July 1, 2021 – when state laws would go into effect – the NCAA was awaiting a decision from the Supreme Court on the *Alston* case. Although it wasn't a case about NIL, it was about the application of antitrust law to college sports. The unanimous decision against the NCAA came in on June 21, 2021, and there's no doubt it impacted the way the NCAA proceeded with its NIL policy.

NCAA NIL Rules

With little time to implement something before some of the state laws went into effect, the NCAA issued an interim NIL policy that went into effect July 1, 2021, providing the following guidance:

- Individuals can engage in NIL activities that are consistent with the law of the state where the school is located. Colleges and universities are responsible for determining whether those activities are consistent with state law.
- College athletes who attend a school in a state without an NIL law can engage in this type of activity without violating NCAA rules related to name, image, and likeness.
- Individuals can use a professional services provider for NIL activities.
- Student-athletes should report NIL activities consistent with state law or school and conference requirements to their school.

A set of frequently asked questions provides further clarity on several issues:

- Prospective student-athletes may participate in the same activities available to current student-athletes without impacting NCAA eligibility; however, these student-athletes should consult

8

The Athlete's NIL Playbook

their state high school athletics association for any questions regarding high school eligibility.

- Student-athletes can enter into agreements with boosters, as long as those agreements comply with state laws and school policies and are not impermissible inducements and do not constitute pay-for-play.

- The NCAA's interim policy specifically does not require student-athletes to report their NIL activities to their schools, but state laws and institutional policies may require it.

- International student-athletes are covered by the interim NIL policy, but they should consult with government agencies for guidance on visa issues and tax implications.

- Reporting of NIL compensation for tax purposes should follow state and country laws.

- The interim NIL policy does not impact a student-athlete's financial aid.

The Evolution of the NCAA's NIL Rules

Since the initial rules were released in July 2021, a number of clarifications have been issued by the NCAA, many of which have been aimed at boosters and NIL collectives. (These are generally groups of boosters/fans who help generate NIL deals/funds for athletes at a specific school, which we'll discuss in Chapter 6.) A timeline and summary is included below to show the evolution of the NIL rules, if you're interested. Otherwise, feel free to jump to Chapter 2, unless you're an international athlete who needs the final section of this chapter about the different rules that apply to you.

- **May 2022:** The focus of this guidance was around the definition of a booster and the type of contact allowed, particularly

9

NIL Rules in College and High School Sports

during recruiting. It defined a booster as "an individual, independent agency, corporate entity (e.g., apparel or equipment manufacturer) or other organization" who promotes an institution's athletics program or provides benefits to enrolled athletes or their family members. Seeking to target the activities of NIL collectives, some of the guidance provided included:

- Boosters/NIL entities cannot communicate with potential student-athletes, their family, or others affiliated with them for recruiting purposes or to encourage enrollment at a particular institution.

- NIL agreements between boosters/NIL entities and prospective student-athletes cannot be guaranteed or promised contingent on initial or continuing enrollment at a particular institution.

- University coaches and staff may not organize or facilitate a meeting between a booster/NIL entity and a prospective student-athlete or communicate with the athlete on the booster/NIL entity's behalf.

- NIL agreements must be based on a case-by-case analysis of the value each athlete brings to the NIL agreement, not as compensation or incentive for enrollment, achievement, or membership on a team.

- **October 2022:** These clarifications centered around what's often referred to as "institutional involvement." It included:

  - **Education and monitoring:** Institutions can and should provide education to athletes, including in areas like financial literacy, taxes, entrepreneurship, and social media. Institutions can also educate collectives and other NIL entities, boosters, and prospective student-athletes.

- **School support for student-athlete NIL activities:** Institutions can hire service providers like marketplaces to inform athletes of potential NIL opportunities. They may also provide stock photos or graphics to the athlete or an outside NIL entity and provide a space for the parties to meet. However, no one within athletics can assist in the execution of the NIL activity, including creating graphics or promotional material, providing equipment (such as a camera or graphic software), or ensuring the athlete completes their obligations. Services such as contract review, tax preparation, and the like also cannot be supplied for free unless they are available to all students.

- **School involvement with collectives/NIL entities:** University personnel, specifically including coaches, can assist with fundraising activities through appearances or by providing autographed memorabilia. However, they cannot donate cash directly to the collective or other entity, and they cannot be employed by, or have an ownership stake in, an outside NIL entity. Schools are also permitted to request that donors provide funds to collectives and other entities, but they cannot request that those funds be directed to a specific sport or student-athlete. Institutions may also provide donor information and facilitate meetings between donors and collectives or other NIL entities.

- **Negotiating revenue sharing and compensation:** Athletics staff members cannot represent athletes for NIL deals, including securing or negotiating deals on behalf of the athlete. Similarly, individuals or entities representing athletics (such as third-party rights holders and third-party agents) cannot represent enrolled athletes for NIL deals, including securing or negotiating those deals. Institutions may not enter into contracts with athletes for the sale of products related to the athlete's NIL, meaning third parties will be necessary to facilitate co-branded product offerings. It was also clarified that coaches and other staff members are also prohibited from providing NIL deals to athletes through their own businesses, which includes a prohibition on coaches paying athletes to promote the coach's camp. Athletes are also prohibited from receiving compensation directly or indirectly for promoting an athletics competition in which they participate.

- The Division I Board of Directors also unanimously adopted a proposal for new allegation and conclusion standards when potential violations related to the interim policy occur. Their summary states, "When information available to the enforcement staff indicates impermissible conduct occurred, the enforcement staff and Committee on Infractions will presume a violation occurred unless the school clearly demonstrates that the behaviors in question were in line with existing NCAA rules and the interim policy." It's essentially a guilty-until-proven-innocent standard.

- **March 2023:** In a letter to universities, the NCAA reminded institutions that they couldn't compensate athletes for NIL, including "entities acting on behalf of the institution," presumably targeting collectives and new fundraising mechanisms proposed by universities to directly pay athletes. The memo also expressly prohibited universities from providing assets to "entities engaged in NIL," such as priority points to stadium seating and access. This memo was sent shortly after Texas A&M announced the 12th Man+ Fund, which would award priority points and take in donations to compensate athletes directly.

- **January 2024:** This new proposal ushered in a number of new changes to the NIL rules:

  - Service providers can voluntarily register in a centralized system to work with student-athletes, helping athletes make informed choices about representation.

  - Athletes must disclose NIL deals worth over $600 within 30 days, including contract terms and compensation. New enrollees must disclose within 30 days of enrollment. Schools report anonymized data to NCAA biannually.

  - NCAA will provide contract templates and guidance on contractual obligations to help athletes and families make informed decisions.

  - NCAA will develop ongoing education and resources about NIL policies, rules, and best practices for athletes and stakeholders.

- **April 2024:** With this proposal, schools were permitted to begin providing assistance to athletes, including identifying and facilitating deals between athletes and third parties. However, in order to take advantage of this assistance, they must disclose to their school information on any NIL deals equal to or greater than $600 in value within 30 days of entering into the agreement. Data from those disclosures will be deidentified and aggregated for trend reporting to the NCAA. Prospective student-athletes must disclose any prior activity within 30 days of enrollment in order to accept school assistance for NIL activities.

Note that more changes are expected in 2025 as revenue sharing begins. Athletes should note two rules here: (1) deals with third parties considered "associated entities or individuals" (which includes certain boosters and all collectives) must be at fair market rates and are subject to challenge in a new neutral arbitration system, and (2) agreements with other third parties must be disclosed if the payment exceeds $600 (in the aggregate if you do receive multiple payments from a brand). The *House* settlement is covered more in Chapter 11.

State laws still continue to evolve as well. For example, in April 2024, Virginia passed a law allowing institutions to pay athletes directly even before the *House* settlement was announced. The law also prohibits the NCAA from penalizing schools that follow the law. Georgia passed a similar law a few months later.

Only a federal law could standardize the rules and laws that govern NIL. Absent that, athletes continue to operate under a patchwork of state laws that often conflict with NCAA rules and guidance.

NAIA Rules

The National Association of Intercollegiate Athletics changed its NIL rules prior to the NCAA, announcing on October 6, 2020, it had passed the first legislation in college sports to allow student-athletes to be compensated for use of their NIL.

Initially, the NAIA said it would allow a student-athlete to "receive compensation for promoting any commercial product, enterprise, or for any public or media appearance." They also specifically allowed for athletes to reference their participation in intercollegiate athletics in promotions and appearances.

At the time, California, Colorado, Florida, and Nebraska had already passed state legislation to allow NIL, with Florida's law set to go into effect July 1, 2021, and the other three states January 1, 2023.

Unlike the NCAA, the NAIA requires disclosure of NIL deals to an athlete's athletic director if the NIL includes a reference to the athlete's status as an athlete or the institution.

NJCAA Rules

The National Junior College Athletic Association followed the NCAA timeline and changed its NIL rules as of July 1, 2021. Similar to the NCAA's rules, it doesn't allow anyone employed by the university to pay athletes directly and does not allow payments contingent on enrollment or athletic performance. The rules require quid pro quo (an exchange of goods or services) and do permit athletes to hire professional service providers for NIL purposes only.

The NJCAA did enact one stipulation the NCAA originally considered: Athletes cannot engage in NIL deals that conflict with the institutions' existing partnerships, sponsorships, or agreements. However, by 2024 this was no longer listed in the NJCAA's bylaws.

Institutional Rules

When the NCAA released its interim rules leading into July 1, 2021, it abandoned the "guardrails" it had previously considered for NIL and instead shifted responsibility to state laws and institutional policies. The University of Florida was the first to release its policy, which included these key aspects:

- Compensation can't be provided in exchange for athletic performance or attendance at UF.

- Opportunities can't conflict with academic or team-related activities.

- Rights must be secured from Gator Sports Properties for use of any university or athletic department marks and logos.

- Prohibited categories include gambling/sports wagering vendors or any vendors associated with athletic performance-enhancing drugs.

- Use of any athletic department facilities will require advance approval, including location agreements, waiver of liability forms, and applicable rental fees.

- All agreements must be disclosed within four days but is expressly not an approval process.

- The term of a contract for representation or compensation for the use of a student-athlete's NIL cannot extend beyond participation in athletics at the institution.

- Representation must be limited to NIL and may not include future professional athletic contract negotiations.

- International student-athletes should get guidance from the University of Florida International Student Center before entering any NIL agreements.

One rule that stood out was with regard to compensation from boosters, which went beyond anything the NCAA implemented. UF's original rule stated, "The University of Florida, the athletic department, staff members or boosters may not compensate or arrange compensation to a current or prospective intercollegiate athlete for her or his name, image, likeness."

At the time, UF was approaching its policy based on its interpretation of the state law,[6] but it's also notable that UF later ended up with the first collective – Gator Collective – as we've come to define collectives (groups of boosters, fans, and other interested parties who form an entity that helps identify and facilitate NIL deals for athletes, usually dedicated to one institution).

Schools scrambled to put together institutional policies, many not planning on having their own separate from the NCAA until the organization abandoned its original guardrails and issued its more simplistic interim policy. It took some schools months to create policies, leaving athletes and the companies who wanted to do deals with them uncertain about what was and wasn't allowed under the rules.

Many schools still have policies in place, and they vary in terms of prohibited categories (such as alcohol and tobacco), the process by which you can ask permission to include the university's intellectual property (such as the school's name or logo) in NIL deals, and use of institutional facilities. You should review your school's current policy before entering into any NIL deals to ensure you're following all the rules.

It should also be noted that athletes at the military service academies are not allowed to participate in NIL deals.

Athletes need to consider current NCAA/NAIA/NJCAA rules, state laws, and institutional policies – in addition to federal laws governing student visas and advertising disclosures, discussed more herein – before entering NIL agreements to ensure compliance with all applicable rules and laws.

High School Rules

High school and youth athletes have additional rules to follow in the form of organizations that govern their sports leagues. For example, the Georgia High School Association creates and enforces rules for hundreds of public institutions and dozens of private institutions within the State of Georgia.

As of the writing of this book, more than three dozen state high school associations have changed their rules to allow NIL in some capacity. Many have restrictions mirroring the early state laws applicable to college athletes, such as restrictions on NIL deals for alcohol, tobacco, CBD, adult entertainment, and more. Many also include restrictions against using school names or logos, not even allowing it with permission from the institution as is allowed widely at the collegiate level.

17

NIL Rules in College and High School Sports

A current index of state high school association NIL rules can be found on the microsite for this book at www.athletesnilplaybook.com/highschool.

Youth Athletes

Assuming any youth sports association you compete within allows it, NIL isn't just for high school or college athletes. In April 2023, Reese Lechner became the youngest-known female to sign an NIL deal at just 10 years old.

Reese's mother, Hannah Lechner, was a college athlete herself, making a run to the Final Four in 2003–2004 while playing basketball at the University of Minnesota. The elder Lechner joined a Facebook group I formed for parents of athletes to ask questions, and it wasn't long before she was putting the same sort of advice you're getting in this book into action to help her daughter achieve her goal of landing an NIL deal before the end of 2023.

"I learned about NIL from my mom, who played college basketball, and I believe NIL can help me and more athletes get exposure to colleges and more opportunities in life," said Reese. "YouTube, TikTok, and Instagram are how most marketing is done for people under the age of 18. Also, I think it would be great to make money before I can actually get an hourly job. My dream school is very expensive, so I want to start saving and will keep working towards a scholarship."

Reese said she started reaching out to brands with products and services she already used, but her first big break was with her local gym, the Performance Center in Stewartville, Minnesota, where she trains for basketball and volleyball.

"I was signing up with my local athletic performance gym, and they asked me to write out goals. I wrote a page about how I wanted to be the youngest female athlete in the nation with an NIL deal, and I told them how I can refer other members in my grade and in the surrounding towns."

That deal helped Reese achieve her goal and came along with some added perks.

"I was really excited to make money for the first time (outside of allowance, of course). More importantly, I thought it was cool to be a leader in NIL. If I can inspire other youth athletes, I want to do that. It was fun to be in the local newspaper, and kids and adults in AAU and Junior Olympic volleyball were asking me about it. I had cameras in the gym watching me work out and even signed a couple autographs."

The elder Lechner says the right age for an athlete to start pursuing NIL opportunities depends on several factors, including their maturity and athletic career trajectory.

"Reese is a mature kid, and my husband and I decided that if she's willing to lead, we'll provide the guidance and direction to accomplish this goal, like any other. There are responsibilities that come with NIL deals, and it is our job to ensure she understands those and upholds her end of the contract. Specifically, because of her age, we support her by monitoring social media, coaching her through the options and setting up virtual or in-person meetings, not unlike an agent. Oh, and since she's 12 (now), driving her to her gym/obligations."

Having navigated this experience with her daughter, Lechner has some advice for other parents of youth athletes:

- **Maturity is key.** "At such a young age, children are still developing physically, mentally, and emotionally, so it's crucial to ensure the child is mature enough to handle the responsibilities and pressures that come with NIL deals, such as managing a public image, dealing with envy/resentment, and fulfilling contractual obligations."

- **Make NIL an educational opportunity.** "Focus on making this an educational and growth opportunity. We have talked about the next level in sports since age 10, and we've visited over a dozen college campuses in person. We talk about changes in the NCAA, NIL, academics, and athletics at the next level as everyday conversation. Reese has many role models at the Division I and II level, and many of them have NIL deals."

- **Understand the legal and regulatory components.** "Trust advisors like Kristi Dosh and do your own research as this is an ever-changing landscape with a lot of misinformation. The worst thing you could do is create a situation where your child becomes ineligible for middle school/high school sports. We contacted our school's athletic director immediately before signing any NIL deals."

- **Expect to hear "no" a lot.** "'No' may not be a 'no' forever. Always ask if you can check back later or if they have any other ideas or leads for your child to pursue."

- **Be open to new things.** "The future belongs to those who are willing to try new things."

Also, remember that you don't have to say yes to every opportunity, either. Lechner said they decided to turn down a deal with a local pizza restaurant.

"As we worked through the details, we figured it was going to be a bit too burdensome and a lot of it would fall on us as parents. The pizza owner was amazing to work with; it just would have been extra driving and time, and she was too busy with her sports schedule, so we turned it down."

Did you notice how I said Reese was the youngest-known female athlete to sign an NIL deal? That's because earlier in 2023, golf bag manufacturer Sunday Golf signed six-year-old Patton Green, the 2022 Southern California State Champion for Six and Under. The company said it was looking to expand its presence in youth golf with the deal.

Reese and Patton don't have huge followings: as of this writing, 525 and 1,943 on Instagram, respectively. But they each bring something unique to the table, and so do you!

International Athletes

If you're an international student-athlete – or planning to be one – you've probably heard about the NIL opportunities that may await you. However, as you prepare for this next chapter, there's something you might not know: Your visa status could severely limit what you can do.

The truth is that for the nearly 25,000 international student-athletes participating in the NCAA, name, image, and likeness is more like a dream rather than a reality. While your American teammates can freely capitalize on NIL, your ability to do the same is heavily restricted not by your university or the NCAA but by U.S. immigration laws.

Although the NCAA placed no restrictions on international athletes, there are restrictions on student visas from the federal government that severely limit the opportunities available to international athletes in the U.S. on F-1 visas.

Typical NIL deals require an athlete to perform a service for compensation (including not only cash payment but also free goods or services), which directly conflicts with immigration policy and work authorization allowed under an F-1 student visa.

"The work authorization that is available to student-athletes is very limited and typically tied to their program of study," said Ksenia Maiorova, an immigration attorney working in the NIL space.[7]

"So, if you're studying microbiology, you may be able to get work authorization to go work in a lab and to test your skills there. There are really two options. Typically, there's training that you can do while you're still in school, and then a postgraduate internship that you can do. In certain circumstances, you can also get need-based emergency work authorization for on-campus employment, but that would be something like working at the library or at the cafeteria. None of these scenarios really cover doing work for an outside sponsor in the NIL context."[8]

Many of the U.S. visa regulations were drafted back in 1952, and most have not been updated since 1986. Unfortunately, this means they can be a bit outdated, particularly when it comes to NIL.

Despite numerous proposed bills to amend the F-1 visa to allow employment authorization for international student-athletes to enter into endorsement contracts for the commercial use of their name, images, and likenesses, lawmakers have provided little to no guidance as of the publication of this book, leaving many still seeking answers to address the most obvious of questions.

What we're left with are passive income opportunities or successfully applying for a different type of visa as the only options for international athletes, both of which we'll discuss in more detail in this chapter.

Types of Visas

Let's start with the types of visas an international athlete can apply for: F-1 visa (Academic Student), P-1A visa (Athlete), and O-1 visa (Individuals with Extraordinary Ability or Achievement).

Visa Type	Definition	Criteria
Student Visa (F-1)	A visa for international students pursuing academic studies in the U.S. (most common)	Must be enrolled full-time in an accredited institution
Professional Athlete Visa (P-1A)	A visa for athletes recognized internationally for their performance	Must submit at least two of the following to demonstrate international recognition: Evidence of having participated to a significant extent in a prior season with a major United States sports league (generally doesn't apply because of NCAA rules, but there's an exception for athletes who've played in the Canadian Hockey League and were not paid more than their actual and necessary expenses) Evidence of participation in international competition with a national team A written statement from an official of the governing body of the sport detailing how the athlete is internationally recognized A written statement from a recognized expert in the sport, or media member, detailing how the athlete is internationally recognized

(continued)

(continued)

Visa Type	Definition	Criteria
		Evidence that the individual or team is ranked if the sport has international rankings
		Evidence that the individual has received a significant honor or award in the sport
		Evidence of having participated to a significant extent in a prior season for a U.S. college or university in intercollegiate competition
Extraordinary Ability Visa (O-1)	A visa for individuals with extraordinary ability or achievement in their field, including athletes	Must demonstrate extraordinary ability through at least three of the following criteria:
		Receipt of nationally or internationally recognized prizes or awards for excellence
		Membership in associations requiring outstanding achievements, as judged by recognized national or international experts
		Published material about the applicant in professional or major trade publications or other major media
		Participation as a judge of the work of others in the field
		Original scientific, scholarly, or artistic contributions of major significance

Visa Type	Definition	Criteria
Employment-Based Visa (EB-1A)	Also known as the "Extraordinary Ability" Green Card	Authorship of scholarly articles in the field, published in professional or major trade publications or other major media
		Display of the applicant's work at artistic exhibitions or showcases
		Performance in a leading or critical role for organizations with distinguished reputations
		Must meet a minimum of three of the following criteria or demonstrate extraordinary ability with a one-time achievement, such as an Olympic Medal:
		Documentation of the alien's receipt of lesser nationally or internationally recognized prizes or awards for excellence in the field of endeavor
		Documentation of the alien's membership in associations in the field for which classification is sought, which require outstanding achievements of their members, as judged by recognized national or international experts in their disciplines or fields

(continued)

(continued)

Visa Type	Definition	Criteria
		Published material about the alien in professional or major trade publications or other major media relating to the alien's work in the field for which classification is sought; such evidence shall include the title, date, and author of the material and any necessary translation
		Evidence of the alien's participation, either individually or on a panel, as a judge of the work of others in the same or an allied field of specification for which classification is sought
		Evidence of the alien's original scientific, scholarly, artistic, athletic, or business-related contributions of major significance in the field
		Evidence of the alien's authorship of scholarly articles in the field, in professional or major trade publications, or other major media

Visa Type	Definition	Criteria
		Evidence that the alien has performed in a leading or critical role for organizations or establishments that have a distinguished reputation
		Evidence that the alien has commanded a high salary or other significantly high remuneration for services in relation to others in the field
		Evidence of commercial successes in the performing arts, as shown by box office receipts or record, cassette, compact disc, or video sales

For far more detail on pursuing P-1A or O-1 visas, I highly recommend the book *National X Immigration* by Maiorova and fellow immigration attorney Amy Maldonado. I'm including some of their expertise and interpretations below, but they are the experts.

One good rule of thumb they recommended when they joined me on my *Business of College Sports* podcast was that athletes have at least $10,000 in NIL deals before deciding to pursue a visa other than the F-1, due to the cost involved with petitioning for the other visas. They estimate that fewer than 5% of international college athletes would qualify for these visas.

P-1A Visas

In order to pursue a P-1A visa, someone other than the athlete must petition on their behalf. Maiorova and Maldonado say this could be the athlete's agent, an NIL sponsor, or a collective. Although it could also be the university, they haven't seen universities willing to get involved at this level.

As part of the application, a detailed description must be provided of the activities the athlete will engage in, including competitions, events, appearances, and other activities required by their NIL deals. The attorneys advise that athletes execute as many NIL deals as possible prior to applying. Although they cannot render the services in the contract while on the F-1 visa, they can execute the contract so the work therein can be included as part of the application.

"An athlete with signed NIL deals is more likely to meet the requirements of the P-1A with respect to documenting future work than someone whose deals are more speculative, not affirmed in writing, and/or not executed by all parties."[9]

The final element required for a P-1A visa is a difficult one for many college athletes because it requires the athlete to be internationally recognized from a reputation perspective. Maiorova and Maldonado believe that, coupled with guidance issued during the Biden administration, athletes from the following sports have an advantage in applying for the P-1A: basketball, football, baseball, track and field, gymnastics, and swimming. The reason? Media coverage, high revenue and attendance, along with the high level of achievement required, make it easier to make a case for athletes in these sports.

In addition to the fees required to pursue a P-1A visa, it can also take up to six months for the ruling on the petition and several weeks to several months for the consular interview (although an athlete may qualify for expedition of the interview).

Kieron Van Wyk was the first golfer, and one of only a handful of international athletes in the first three years of NIL, to receive a P-1A visa.

Before Van Wyk was approved for the P-1A visa, his agent, Christian Addison – founder of Addison Sports and Entertainment – said they could only focus on deals that could be completed outside of the United States.

"This meant flying Kieron abroad to meet with brands or attend events. This strategy enabled him to benefit from NIL opportunities without breaching U.S. immigration laws. However, it was costly and time-consuming, underscoring the disparities and additional hurdles international athletes face compared to their domestic peers."[10]

More than 85 brands had pursued Van Wyk by mid-2024. Addison, his agent, said that not being able to build relationships with brands as a college golfer would disadvantage a player like Van Wyk compared to his domestic peers, who could start earlier, while the P-1A levels the playing ground.

"The first aspect to the equation is the financial piece: When you are battling to make the PGA Tour, you're losing money every week," said Addison. "You have tournament fees, travel fees, your day-to-day expenses, then any coaching you have, whether it's a swing coach, sports performance coach, or otherwise. And even if you're placing at the top of every tournament, it's an expensive sport to stay afloat until you achieve the level of the Tour. Brands you partner with can assist in that and sometimes are able to keep you afloat long enough for you to achieve your dreams."

Addison says relationships with brands are everything in golf.

"It distinguishes you from your peers and shapes your career in whichever companies and causes you choose to partner with. If you're an international athlete in college and performing well, you're not able to partner with brands right now. Someone substantially below you could get that deal simply because they're an American. And that means years of building a relationship with that brand so when they do try and turn pro, the brand knows them as opposed to someone who just graduated college and is not American. It puts you at a massive disadvantage when you're not able to build relationships with sponsors during your formative years who could be the difference in you surviving as a professional golfer one day."

Van Wyk chose not to go the expedited route for his P-1A application due to the added expense and because the immigration office indicated they were less busy than usual. Addison said it only took about ten weeks to receive their response.

However, receiving a P-1A visa is no easy task. As of late 2024, LSU women's basketball athlete Last-Tear Poa had filed a lawsuit in the Middle District of Louisiana against U.S. Citizenship and Immigration Services after her P-1A application was denied.

USCIS director Tracy Tarango argued that Poa and her representation "failed to prove not only that she was present in the U.S. solely to play basketball, but also that her desire to capitalize off her NIL is related to her athletic career – not just to her individual financial gain."[11]

Poa is the first known collegiate athlete to challenge the USCIS in federal court over lost NIL opportunities.

O-1A Visa

While the P-1A visa is for "internationally recognized" athletes, the O-1A visa is a step higher, requiring "extraordinary ability." This above-ordinary ability must be demonstrated by sustained national or international achievement, including meeting at least three of the criteria outlined in the table above.

Like the P-1A, the O-1A is required to be filed by a U.S. petitioner, which can be a U.S. company engaging the services of the athletes, or an agent petitioner. As a practical matter, potential petitioners include NIL agencies, collectives, or the brand sponsors directly.

Northwestern State's Hansel Emmanuel, a men's basketball athlete who only has one arm, received approval for an O-1 visa in 2022. He's the only known international athlete to receive his visa, although he has since lost it for unpublicized reasons.[12]

EB-1A Visa

The biggest difference between the other types of visas and the EB-1A is that the latter is a way to get a green card without a job offer from a U.S. company. An athlete who demonstrates extraordinary ability can also petition for an EB-1A visa. Unlike the O-1A and P-1A, this category allows the athlete to self-petition. While the EB-1A visa has some criteria that look similar to those of the O-1A, there are some additional categories of permissible evidence and subtle differences between categories in the O-1A that sound similar to the EB-1A. For example, signed NIL contracts are helpful for the P-1A and O-1A, but the EB-1A Salary or Renumeration criterion requires evidence of income received, which would be illegal for Canadian hammer thrower Camryn Rogers under an F-1 visa. For an EB-1A, the athlete must also show they will continue to compete in the U.S. and that it will benefit the U.S.

Rogers, represented by Maiorova, was the first known case of a collegiate athlete being approved for an EB-1A visa during the NIL era. Maiorova says in her book that Camryn had a good case because of her high world ranking and achievements at the highest levels of international competition.

There's a more detailed case study of Rogers's case in Maiorova and Maldonado's book, but here is a brief outline of the criteria that were submitted for her: She had performance at the U20 World Championships, the Canadian National Championship, and the NCAA National Championship for the Awards criterion; articles about her in *Sports Illustrated*, *The Toronto Star*, and *Track & Field News* for the Publications criterion; making an Olympic team gave her something for the Membership criteria; her NCAA record could be used for the Leading Role criterion; and her full athletic scholarship for the Salary or Renumeration criterion.

Rogers had a world ranking, several records, and was the number-one-ranked hammer thrower in Canada when her application was submitted, giving her a strong case. Her application was approved in just 10 days, with no additional information requested.

She was also granted her green card within six months, making her a permanent resident of the United States. This not only allows for NIL deals, but also employment and the ability to stay even after her collegiate career to continue to work with coaches in the United States as she transitions to a professional career.

Limitations on NIL for International Athletes

Assuming you're not one of the few international athletes who will be able to acquire a different type of visa, let's talk about what you can do under your F-1 visa.

The primary challenge for international student-athletes under visa restrictions is distinguishing between "active" and "passive" income-generating NIL activities. It's an important distinction, because international athletes can only engage in passive income-generating activities while on U.S. soil under an F-1 visa.

"Active" income-generating activities would be considered "employment" under the F-1 visa and are defined as being compensated for rendering a service or producing a product which benefits another person or company. These activities are not allowed for international athletes on the F-1 visa while in the U.S., although they can participate in these activities while in their home country or in another country that allows it under its own visa rules.

"Passive" income-generating opportunities, which are allowable on the F-1 visa while in the U.S., allow athletes to receive compensation for use of their NIL but do not require the athlete to actively promote or support the effort.

Maiorova and Maldonado have joined me on my podcast multiple times, and we've gone through some common scenarios playing out in the NIL economy to demonstrate the difference between active and passive activities.[13]

Scenario #1: Activating NIL Deals in the Athlete's Home Country

Scenario: You sign an NIL deal while in the United States and agree to create the content and post to your social media while in your home country for winter break.

Advice: Both lawyers agree that athletes can sign NIL deals while in the U.S. and then activate (create the content and promote it) in their home country. However, the ladies warn that in a consular interview, you may find it tough to prove that you posted while home unless you're, say, a British athlete posting a photo in front of Big Ben so that there's no question you were in your home country.

Outcome: Permissible

Scenario #2: Licensing Deal (Group, Apparel, Trading Cards, NFTs, etc.)

Scenario: An outside company wants to license your NIL for use on apparel, goods, or NFTs.

Advice: If the company does all the creation, marketing, and promotion for the product, while you (the athlete) do nothing to promote or market, the ladies agree it would be deemed passive income. This means the athlete cannot post about the products on social media (not even resharing the company's content), verbally promote, or otherwise bring attention to it while on U.S. soil.

Technically, the athlete could promote while in their home country, but the same advice applies as above in terms of making it undeniable where you were located when you participated in the activity.

We'll talk more about group licensing in Chapter 7.

Outcome: Permissible

Scenario #3: Paying International Athletes Outside of the U.S. for Work in the U.S.

Scenario: A company wants you to promote their product via social media while in the U.S. but promises to pay you in your home country's currency and bank in order to get around F-1 rules.

Advice: Amy says it's clear this is not allowed. "Under United States immigration regulations any services that are rendered in the U.S. – regardless of whether they're paid for inside the U.S. or outside the U.S. (in any currency) … are typically subject to compensation. That is work, period."

Outcome: Not Permissible

Scenario #4: Donating NIL Money to Charity

Scenario: You are paid by your university's collective to participate in a charity event and you agree to donate your compensation to charity.

Advice: More than one international athlete has publicly announced NIL deals where they're donating the compensation to charity, presumably to get around F-1 rules. Unfortunately, Maiorova says that doesn't work.

"In order to donate money, one has to have title to the money, and the moment a student-athlete acquires title to the money – if it's on the basis of doing something – then we have a work authorization problem."

Outcome: Not Permissible

Scenario #5: Hiring a Social Media Manager to Post

Scenario: As a student-athlete, you hire an outside individual to run your social media account and post for you in order to get around the F-1 rules.

34

The Athlete's NIL Playbook

Advice: Maldonado pointed out that she has advised clients that if they have a U.S. work-authorized social media manager, that person can post on the international athlete's social media without any issues. However, there are a few caveats here:

- You cannot pose in the photo or put out scripted content because that crosses the line and makes the activity no longer passive.
- When you get in front of a consular officer, you'd need to prove who pressed the button to post on social media, which Maldonado thinks could be difficult to prove.

Outcome: Permissible but dependent on the consular officer (with the recommendation not to do this)

Scenario #6: Doing NIL Deals While in Another Country

Scenario: Your team is attending a tournament or in another country (not your home country) and you promote NIL deals for U.S.-based companies.

Advice: Maiorova says this may or may not be permissible, depending on the country where you're attempting to do the work.

"Just because you're not within the U.S. immigration system doesn't mean you can work without authorization in the Bahamas. They have their own immigration laws. They have their own employment authorization requirements. You can't just assume because you're admitted to go there on vacation you can do things that are revenue-generating activities."

Outcome: Permissible by the U.S., but you must also check that it's permissible under the laws of the country where you're doing the work

Former Kentucky men's basketball athlete Oscar Tshiebwe was one of the first, and most publicized, international athletes to take advantage of time out of the U.S. to complete NIL deals. In August 2022, Kentucky's basketball team traveled to the Bahamas to play four exhibition games, and Tshiebwe created content for $500,000 in NIL deals while he was there.

According to a report from *The Athletic*, Tshiebwe did photo shoots, ad reads, and merchandise signings for four different companies. He also shot more generic photos and videos brands can buy later to use.[14]

Weighing the Risks

Unfortunately, navigating NIL opportunities as an international athlete ultimately boils down to your risk tolerance because of the lack of clear guidance from the federal government on these issues. Opinions on what is permissible can vary from one attorney to the next, and the consequences can be severe.

Maldonado says she advises her clients very conservatively, "because no one has an entitlement to a visa."

She also notes, "There is something called the doctrine of consular non-renewability. If you get a State Department officer who thinks you worked without authorization, and they don't want to renew your student visa, they don't have to, and there's nothing you can do about it."

The reality is the average review time by a consular officer is roughly 90 seconds. These officers don't have time to pursue the nuance and figure out whether or not something is legal. Many times, these decisions are based on a gut reaction: They like it or they don't like it.

Any finding of ineligibility, or inconsistent intent and activity, can be grounds for denying future visa applications. Because there is no appeal process (meaning the consular officer's decision is final), Maiorova and Maldonado don't think it's worth it to take risks when it comes to activities that straddle the line between passive and active.

What's Next for International Athletes

Unfortunately, no one knows what's next for international athletes. At the time of this writing (four years into NIL), the federal government has offered no guidance for international athletes on permissible and impermissible NIL activities.

What we do know is that no one is stopping you from building your brand, activating NIL deals within your home country, or seeking out passive opportunities. While limiting in comparison to your American teammates, these steps will certainly better position you if changes do arise.

But most importantly, regardless of the scenario, please assess the risk and consult an immigration attorney with experience in NIL. Violations of your immigration status can have lifelong effects with very few actions for recourse. Any finding of ineligibility, or inconsistent intent and activity, can be grounds for denying future visa applications.

Resources and news for international athletes navigating NIL is available at https://www.nilforinternationalathletes.com.

Key Takeaways

- NIL stands for "name, image, and likeness" and refers to the right of athletes to earn money through activities using their personal brand.
- Athletes attending schools in the NAIA, NCAA, and NJCAA all have the right to monetize their NIL, but each organization has its own rules that must be followed.
- High school and youth athletes can only monetize their NIL if they're in a state that allows it. For the latest information, visit www.athletesnilplaybook.com/highschool.

37

NIL Rules in College and High School Sports

- Even youth athletes can monetize NIL in many cases, but parental guidance, maturity considerations, and compliance with school/league rules are essential.
- International athletes face significant limitations due to visa restrictions. Most F-1 visa holders can only participate in "passive" NIL activities while in the U.S.
- Before entering any NIL deal, understand how it might affect your eligibility under all applicable rules – athletic organization, state law, school policy, and visa status if relevant.

Chapter 2

NIL Activities and Opportunities

I've written about, and served on panels with, athletes from every division who were able to leverage their NIL even with moderately sized social media platforms. One of my favorite stories is Division III women's volleyball athlete Laney Higgins.

When I first met Higgins, she had just become the first female high school athlete in Florida to sign an NIL deal. At the time, Florida's state high school association didn't allow NIL deals, but she had finished her high school eligibility and signed a deal with Q30 Innovations, a company that produces devices to reduce brain injuries.

It didn't matter that Higgins's following hovered around 1,300 at the time, or that she wasn't a household name committed to a Division I institution. Higgins was then, and is now, proactive about reaching out to companies and working her connections.

Higgins has now worked with multiple brand partners, including local businesses near the Brookhaven, Georgia, campus of Oglethorpe University and national companies like Champs, Outback, Quest Nutrition, and CeraVe. Perhaps her most exciting deal to date, however, is with Lululemon, a brand at the top of many athletes' wish lists, which we'll talk about later on in this chapter.

The point is that many myths circulate about NIL, but some of the most damaging write off the market as only existing for a few:

NIL is only for male athletes.
Only Division I athletes get NIL deals.
You need a big social media following to take advantage of NIL.

Fortunately for the athletes (and parents) reading this, none of this is true.

So, now that we've dispensed with the falsehoods, let's look at all the different ways athletes can monetize their NIL.

Social Media Marketing

The most popular type of NIL deal is social media marketing. When new NIL rules went into effect in 2020 (NAIA) and 2021 (NCAA and NJCAA), most of the deals announced on the first day were brands compensating athletes in exchange for social media posts on Instagram, Snapchat, TikTok, Twitter (now X), and YouTube.

As mentioned in the introduction, former NAIA volleyball athlete Chloe Mitchell has the distinction of being the first college athlete ever to monetize her NIL due to the NAIA's rule change in 2020 ahead of the NCAA. Growing her following from double digits to more than two million during the pandemic allowed her to work with brands already sliding into her DMs.

Mitchell was able to work with brands like Target, Walmart, and Ford for social media content in her first year of NIL. When she realized she was learning more about business firsthand through her brand partnerships than she was in classes – and was making six figures – Mitchell made the decision to become a full-time creator and entrepreneur, roles she's still thriving in today as she continues to work with brands from the brand new house she bought with her NIL money at just 20 years old.

When we talk about NCAA athletes and NIL, two of the most visible college athletes on July 1, 2021, when new NCAA NIL rules became effective, were basketball-playing identical twins Haley and Hanna Cavinder, who've since built an empire around their joint brand as the "Cavinder Twins." Not only were they among the first to announce deals on that monumental day in college sports history, but they did so in grand fashion on a billboard in Times Square.

From there, the Cavinder Twins went on to earn more than $2 million from NIL deals in the first year of exercising their new rights, which included social media posts, merchandise, and even equity stakes.

Then there's the most-followed college athlete at the beginning of the NIL era: LSU gymnast Olivia Dunne. I had the pleasure of reporting on her first NIL deal in September 2021 with Vuori activewear brand, and at the time she had a combined 5.7 million followers on TikTok and Instagram. Not surprisingly, she easily became a seven-figure earner, with many of her deals relying on social media content.

Enough about the stars. I'm sure it's no surprise they can make money. But what about the athlete with 5,000 followers? Or 2,500?

Let's get back to Higgins. How did a DIII athlete with a moderate following attract a national brand that was doing very little in the NIL space despite the number of athletes who would line up to work with them? It's all thanks to her weekly W4alking & T4lking series on Instagram Live, where Higgins talks to another college athlete while they walk across campus to class. She created the series as a result of her

41

NIL Activities and Opportunities

experience in Meta's Empower 2.0 program (where she was the only DIII athlete selected from hundreds of applicants), thanks to an educational session that suggested developing a weekly Instagram Live series.

I was a coach in the program during the same cohort as Higgins, and I have to applaud her not only for taking the advice but also for sticking with it even though I'm sure her watching audience was small in the beginning. Most of the athletes in the cohort gave up on it, but Higgins persisted. It would take more than a year for Lululemon to come calling, but Higgins says it was worth it:

> *My dream brand to collaborate with has always been Lululemon, so to have them partner with me on what has been their first national female NIL campaign has been amazing. I'm so grateful that Lululemon not only sees the value in working with a small school student-athlete like myself, but that they're so ultra supportive of W4lking and T4lking's mission of showcasing other female student-athletes from around the country, who are doing great things both in and out of their sport.*

Thanks to her ongoing efforts to grow her brand and engagement, Higgins now has more than 30,000 followers across her social media channels.

Although the details of Higgins's story are unique, her ability to monetize her NIL even as a small school athlete with a modest following is not. In later chapters, you'll meet a Division III football athlete with a four-figure following who did nearly 40 deals in his first year of NIL, a DII track athlete who put off a pro career to learn how to leverage his NIL, and many more who've successfully landed social media marketing deals with modest followings.

Important: FTC Requirements

Federal law requires that you disclose any financial, employment, personal, or family relationship with a brand. The Federal Trade Commission requires that this disclosure be placed within the endorsement message, meaning it needs to be in your caption on social media.

The FTC's guidance says your disclosure shouldn't be mixed into a group of hashtags or links, "on an ABOUT ME or a profile page, at the end of posts or videos, or anywhere that requires a person to click MORE."

If your endorsement is in a picture or video, the FTC advises that you superimpose the disclosure over the picture or video and give viewers enough time to read it. For videos, the guidance is to include it not only in the description of the video but also in the video itself in both audio and visual formats. In a livestream, you should make the disclosure repeatedly.

Here are some ways the FTC says you can disclose your relationship with a brand:

- Thanking the brand for giving you free product
- Using terms like "advertisement," "ad," "sponsored," "[brand name] partner," and "[brand name] ambassador"

- Using hashtags like #ad or #sponsored, but remember the advisement above that it shouldn't be in a big group of hashtags

The FTC says you shouldn't use abbreviations or shorthand like "sp," "spon," "collab," or "ambassador."

You also can't talk about your experience with a product you haven't tried or say something was great just because you got paid to talk about it. This goes beyond FTC advice; it's good advice for ensuring your audience can trust you and continues to take your recommendations.

Last, steer clear of any claims that a product can do something you or the brand can't prove, such as saying it's proven to treat a health condition.

Affiliate and Ambassador Roles

Intricately tied in with social media marketing are affiliate and ambassador roles. Although they may look similar in your Instagram feed, they're not exactly the same.

An ambassador is someone who serves as the face of the brand. They're likely to post behind-the-scenes-type content, and there will be storytelling around the brand. The athletes are typically paid at least some cash in addition to product.

Affiliates are a little different, especially in terms of the way they are compensated. Generally, affiliates are given a personalized link or code to share with their followers. The athlete then receives a commission when someone makes a purchase using their link or code.

Unfortunately, some brands use these terms interchangeably. I've seen many NIL programs by brands labeled as "ambassador" programs when they're really just affiliate structures. And I find that for many athletes, affiliate programs don't make sense.

That's because making impactful money with affiliate programs requires a lot of time and content. There are influencers out there who make their full-time living on affiliate platforms like Amazon and LIKEtoKNOW.it (LTK), but they're usually posting content multiple times a day. I have yet to meet an athlete who has time to produce content at that volume.

However, an affiliate deal might still make sense if it's for a brand you already use that shows up in your content regularly, such as if you wear the same brand of activewear in much of your content already. Or something like LTK might make sense if you already share your #OOTD every day.

General Booty, a quarterback who played for Oklahoma and then University of Louisiana – Monroe, did a commission-based deal with Rock 'Em Socks, which also included an upfront payment for a photo shoot. Asked about when a commission-based deal makes sense, he had this advice:

> *If it is not a big brand name you are super familiar with, look them up and get familiar with their product, mission, and values to see if it fits your brand and what you want to represent. If you know the structure of your NIL deal is commission-based, you have to put into perspective the size of the company and how much business they do versus the percentage you would make off a sale. If it is a small, local hometown business that you have grown up supporting, maybe you take the deal because of what it means to you, but in the back of your head you understand you may not make much off commission but it is still worth it because that business is something you want to be a part of and help them grow.*

Jack Betts, who was a Division III football athlete when NIL began, said he's done multiple affiliate deals. He views those deals as passive income opportunities: "What led to a lot of my success in having that as a passive income type of opportunity was not flooding my timeline and overwhelming all of my followers with the types of branded content that is required as deliverables for some of these partnerships."

Instead, Jack tried to work that content in more organically. "I'd casually work them into posts every now and then, whether it be story posts or some of them would require in-feed as well. But I think it was really important for me to find that balance."

Booty says he also tries to balance his posting for affiliate deals:

I usually post something two to three times initially that first week and continue to put something up once a week for the next couple of weeks. What I have found that I like to do as well is repost pictures of the people that are supporting you and buying your merchandise that are going on social media and posting it and tagging me. I think it's a cool way to show your appreciation to the people that are supporting you and something different a lot of people don't do.

Jack points out that you might want to limit your obligations during your season so you can focus more on your sport and less on keeping up with content creation. Ultimately, he said the passive income could be anywhere from $10 to $120 a month for him, plus many of them had free product included up front or a small cash payment.

As with other types of NIL activities, you want to weigh the pros and cons and figure out how to monetize your NIL without adding more work than necessary to your already full plate.

Lessons, Camps, and Clinics

Not interested in social media marketing? Another type of NIL activity that any athlete can engage in is offering lessons or being part of camps and clinics. In fact, many athletes were already doing this for free prior to NIL. Now they can finally make money.

Football, baseball, basketball, lacrosse, wrestling, and field hockey are just some of the sports where athletes have already hosted camps to leverage and monetize their NIL. Most athletes choose to partner with a gym, YMCA, or other sports facility to minimize their administrative burden. Lessons, camps, and clinics all necessitate certain legal and insurance considerations, so it's usually easier for athletes to partner with a facility or coach that already has policies and procedures in place for those things.

At the end of this section, I've provided a brief overview of some considerations if you plan to host your own event.

Before we get to that, let's talk about what athlete-hosted camps and clinics have looked like. Former Penn State women's basketball player Anna Camden partnered with the YMCA of Centre County to host a basketball camp in September 2022, Camp Camden. More than 50 athletes attended the camp, and Camden donated the $2,500 proceeds to a charity. It was important to her to keep the camp affordable for the families and also to support her charitable partners.

NIL collectives (discussed more in Chapter 7) have also stepped in to help athletes host and profit from camps and clinics. They handle the marketing, facilities rental, and everything else so the athlete only has to show up and coach. Most then funnel 80–90% of the profits back to the athletes involved.

Remember when I said you could engage in NIL activities that support your future career ambitions? Cate Urbani, a cross country and track and field athlete at Baylor University, is a great example of an athlete turning an NIL opportunity into a great foundation for her future career. Urbani began by doing one-on-one and semi-private training sessions for youth runners through Student-Athlete.co, a platform that helps athletes monetize training and lessons:

> What's really awesome about the way Student-Athlete.co works is that I'm not only serving as a coach to these young children, but also building a relationship as a mentor. The children I've taught are usually between third and fifth grade, which are fundamental years in their development. Each kid is so different, and I've learned to be creative with lessons. One young boy I taught thought he could never run more than two laps. One day the track was closed so we decided to "explore" Waco, and he ended up running for over 30 minutes and fell in love. It was such an awesome experience.

Urbani said the onboarding process with Student-Athlete.co was straightforward. She submitted to a background check, was interviewed, and had a call about how to prepare for lessons, along with receiving some resources to help her create a lesson plan. Before each lesson, she receives an email with the athlete's age, interests, and other information.

"I approach each lesson very individually, and will follow up with the parents on goals beforehand if needed, or ask before the lesson. You have to be pretty adaptable and creative, especially when the students/children are below 13 and they each have a different way of learning and engaging their focus."

Building on this foundation, Urbani also started a new role with a community nonprofit, Mission Waco, as a fitness and activities coach in the spring of 2024. When she needed an internship for her major, she reached out to a running program in Colorado and spent the

48

The Athlete's NIL Playbook

summer of 2024 as their first intern and assistant coach. "Through the money I've earned through Student-athlete.co and the sessions I've done, I was able to afford the summer internship experience – which was a whole other incredible experience."

Camps and clinics can also be good options if you only have time for an occasional event, but what if you want to work with youth athletes more often? Private or group lessons in your community are an option. You can contact local youth leagues and ask how you can make your information available to their athletes, or look for newsletters, message boards, and other online platforms like CoachUp where you can post about your services.

There are even online platforms like CoachTube that allow you to coach by video and messaging, or create your own courses, so you don't have to commit to a specific day or time or be restricted to your local area.

Solo Planning Checklist

Now for the boring (but incredibly important!) stuff. Here's a list of things you need to take into consideration or plan for if you are going to attempt lessons, camps, or clinics on your own:

- **Limited Liability Company (LLC):** Consider meeting with an attorney to discuss forming an LLC, which can protect your personal assets from a lawsuit. When done correctly, an LLC will limit any judgments against the company for anything from an accident involving your participants to the assets of the LLC.

- **Insurance:** Consider meeting with an insurance broker or agent to discuss the type of insurance you need for your event or lessons. You might need general liability insurance, accidental medical insurance, or other types to protect you and your participants.

- **Liability waiver:** You should have an attorney draft a liability waiver for your participants to sign saying they understand the potential risks of injuries involved in your event or lessons. Remember, if you're working with athletes under 18, you'll need their parent or guardian to sign this waiver.

- **Facility arrangements:** You'll need somewhere to conduct your lesson, camp, or clinic. Even if you're planning to use a public outdoor space, it's still wise to check with the owner (likely the city or county government) to clear your activity and find out any rules that apply to your usage. You may need to reserve the space, even if it's public. With a private facility, you'll definitely have to reserve it and probably pay a fee. Make sure you get a written contract reserving your day/time and listing all fees, cleanup procedures, waiver requirements, and any other details discussed.

- **Equipment needs:** Although participants will likely bring their own bats, balls, gloves, and so on, you may have other equipment needs. Think about how your lesson or camp/clinic will play out and make a list of everything you'll need. Check with the facility to see if they have anything you can use or look for sponsors for anything you have to purchase.

- **Marketing plan:** Strategize about how people will find out about your lesson, camp, or clinic. Write out a plan for how you will market your services (social media, websites, newsletters, fliers, etc.) and figure out when you will begin your promotion, leaving yourself enough time to get the word out and fill your available spots.

- **Planning for unexpected security, medical, or other emergency situations:** At a minimum, you should invest in a first-aid kit to have on hand. However, you should also think through possible scenarios. For example, if you're planning to

50

The Athlete's NIL Playbook

host a camp outside, what will you do if it rains? If it's unexpectedly hot or cold? If the heat index is dangerously high, you might need to purchase additional water to have on hand for campers. Even if you're hosting alone, you can learn a lot from talking to coaches or trainers who've hosted similar lessons or events and finding out how they prepare and the unexpected circumstances they've had to address.

- **Additional staff or volunteers:** Can you manage 20 eight-year-olds on your own? Spoiler alert: The answer is no. You're being entrusted with the safety and security of your campers, and you need to ensure you have enough people to be able to keep an eye on everyone for safety purposes but also to provide them with the instruction they expected. If you try to coach 20 children on your own for two hours, they may not be getting enough individual attention to feel like they got their money's worth. You can trade favors with teammates and work each other's events or offer assistants a share of your proceeds.

- **Planning out expenses and pricing your services:** It would be a shame to put in all the work required for a camp or clinic only to find out your expenses exceed your revenue. Start with an expense budget, factoring in the expenses you'll incur as outlined in this checklist, and then estimate how many attendees you think you'll have. Again, talking to others who've done similar events can help with this. From there, you can figure out how much you'll need to charge per participant in order to profit from the event. For private lessons, you'll have fewer expenses, so your hourly rate should reflect what makes it "worth it" for you. Check other rates in your area to make sure you're not underpricing yourself but are also competitively priced.

51

NIL Activities and Opportunities

If that sounds like a lot of work or you're tempted to skip steps, consider partnering with an established coach or facility who takes care of these things for you instead of going at it alone. Even in that case, however, you should have an agreement between yourself and the coach or facility to ensure you're receiving the same legal and insurance protections covered above.

Appearances and Autographs

Local businesses near campuses across the country have taken advantage of the new rules around NIL to compensate athletes for appearances at their locations to help draw in customers. Restaurants were some of the first to take advantage of new NIL rules and begin partnering with college athletes. Although many of these deals rely on social media content, there are also in-person components to many of them.

Spencer Sanders, quarterback for Oklahoma State, reached out to local favorite Eskimo Joe's about creating a T-shirt collaboration. To support the new partnership, Sanders then did a meet-and-greet at the restaurant that included autograph signings.[1]

National chains have been in on the action, too. Raising Cane's, which has locations across the United States, has worked with numerous college athletes. One of their most widely publicized personal appearances was with former UGA quarterback Stetson Bennett. Only a few days after leading his team to a national championship, fans were surprised when they got served by Bennett at a local Athens location.[2]

Boost Mobile hosted six player meet-and-greets at locations in key markets during their 2021–2022 campaign. Then–Gonzaga men's basketball athlete Drew Timme was on hand for a Thanksgiving giveaway at a location in Spokane, Washington.

If you need to make the case to a brand, you can share data from Boost Mobile to make your case that athletes can increase engagement both online and in-store.

I wrote on the campaign for *Forbes*, and Boost Mobile reported that the event location ranked number one in the market during the month of November 2021, with a 54% month-over-month increase in sales and a 79% year-over-year increase. Online, a Facebook post for the event resulted in 6,564 impressions, 143 clicks, 21 shares, and 38 positive interactions. Over on Instagram, Timme's amplification post resulted in 1,656 views and 34 comments.

UCLA quarterback Chase Griffin also made an appearance at a Boost Mobile store during the 2021 holiday season. Kids could take photos with Griffin and Santa, and even got free gifts, including an autographed Chase Griffin Boost Mobile Player Card and a limited-edition T-shirt inspired by Griffin's clothing brand BE11IEVE – a great activation that allowed Griffin to promote his own business at the same time.

Boost Mobile said the Los Angeles location had its top-selling day for December 2021 with Griffin's appearance, resulting in an 11% increase in sales month-over-month. His Facebook post received 3,386 impressions, 36 clicks, 21 shares, and 48 positive interactions, and his amplification post on Instagram garnered another 1,522 views.

"Having these local heroes visit a Boost store near campus can increase sales in that location by almost 200%," said Boost Mobile CEO Steven Stokols. "In addition, social posts and awareness driven by our college athletes have increased sales in local college markets where they play."[3]

Many appearances include athletes signing autographs. However, athletes can also get paid for their autograph in virtually any other setting, from selling their own autographed merchandise to charging

NIL Activities and Opportunities

to sign photographs at events. For example, former Alabama softball pitcher Montana Fouts sold autographed softballs on her own website for $55.00 each back in 2022 ($65 now that she's a professional softball player).

It's not just football athletes making the appearances, either. Several members of the UF gymnastics team were contracted through a former NIL collective for UF, the Gator Collective, to make an appearance at a local escape room to promote it.

That same collective, along with many others, also regularly host fan fest events and tailgates where athletes interact with fans, sign autographs, take photos, and more. ICON, a collective for the University of Illinois, hosted a football tailgate during the 2023 season that featured men's and women's basketball players mingling with fans and signing autographs.

We'll talk more about how you can work with collectives, booster clubs, and other third parties in Chapter 7.

Merchandise and Memorabilia

Some of the first companies to pop up in the NIL space in 2021 were platforms to help athletes create their own merchandise, mainly T-shirts. The NIL Store, powered by Campus Ink and backed by Mark Cuban, is just one of the many options athletes have for creating their own apparel without the need to launch their own website or store and ship the merchandise.

This is another type of NIL monetization that DIII volleyball athlete Higgins has taken advantage of, becoming the first DIII athlete to sign with NIL Store in 2022. She designed a hoodie in honor of National Girls & Women in Sports Day, donating a portion of her proceeds to the Women in Sports Foundation. An even bigger success story is that the initial batch sold out quickly.

In January 2024, NIL Store announced it had paid out more than $1 million to college athletes who've sold merchandise on the platform. Because NIL Store has licenses for more than 100 institutions, athletes at those institutions are able to create co-branded merchandise that includes their own name, image, slogan, or trademarks alongside their school name or logo.

"Teaming up with the NIL Store has been one of my favorite collaborations," said Alabama softball athlete Bailey Dowling, NIL Store's first signed female athlete. "One of the many challenges that student-athletes face is time management due to our busy schedules. The Campus Ink NIL Store made the process easy by listening to my ideas and providing timely feedback, as well as results."[4]

Platforms have also been developed to help athletes sell signed memorabilia. For example, Top Tier Authentics released an exclusive collection of officially licensed merchandise signed by players from Georgia, Michigan, and Tennessee football in the Amazon Fanshop in late 2023. Each piece of merchandise included a unique QR code that gives the purchaser access to a video of the athlete signing the item and additional content related to the item.

Other athletes have chosen to sell their merchandise on their own websites. Booty says he uses Printful to design, sell, and ship the merchandise he features on GeneralBootyShop.com. His graphic tees have phrases like "Booty Call" and "General Booty Reporting for Duty."

"When promoting my merchandise, it has been most effective for me to put it on my social media platforms," said Booty. "I have found it is good to post product a few times throughout the first few weeks and then be able to add new product occasionally as well to keep people interested."

Some athletes have even been thinking outside the box when it comes to creating their own merchandise. Former UF gymnast Leah Clapper made history shortly after the NIL rules changed by creating the first-ever gymnastics board game. From figuring out how to produce a physical board game to learning about distribution channels, sales funnels, email newsletters, and more, Clapper successfully sold out the first round of production on her game and was featured in media outlets nationwide for her unique use of her NIL.

When it comes to merchandise and products, the sky is the limit for athletes. So if you're a creative type, feel free to think outside the box!

Group Licensing and Team-Wide Deals

Even if you're not an athlete with a creative streak, merchandise opportunities may come to you through group licensing deals. These are deals where a company wants to work with a group of student-athletes. These athletes may or may not be on the same team or even at the same school.

The most common group licensing deals in NIL involve a company getting the rights to a university's intellectual property alongside that of a group of athletes so they can produce jerseys, shirzees (T-shirt jerseys), trading cards, video games, and other merchandise.

For group licensing deals, you'll usually be contacted by either the brand or a third-party company that specializes in this area, such as the Brandr Group or OneTeam Partners. You'll opt into the deal and then receive royalties based on sales. In some deals, everyone is paid equal amounts, while in others your revenue is dependent on sales specific to you, such as in the case of jerseys or shirzees bearing your name and number. (We'll dive into group licensing more in Chapter 7.)

Team-wide deals have also been common since the inception of NIL. These can be done outside of group licensing and may result in players each being paid individual amounts. Athletes might be asked to promote the brand on social media, appear at an event, participate in a team photoshoot, or another way to provide the quid pro quo required of all NIL deals.

NFTs

Non-fungible tokens (NFTs) were the basis of many NIL deals in the first year or two, although the market has shifted some. These digital assets often take the form of trading cards or autographed photos, and many companies producing them license the intellectual property from the university so players can appear in uniform.

One of the most successful NFT plays was put together by the Players' Lounge, founded by former UGA football players Ty Frix, Keith Marshall, and Aaron Murray. Using a Discord channel to connect fans, the platform released an NFT collection called DGD Mafia in January 2022.

Fans who purchased the NFTs gained access to exclusive content and experiences, both within the online platform and in physical locations. Fifty percent of the profits were designated for the athletes involved. The NFTs ultimately sold out, with each athlete earning $28,000.

Podcasts, Radio, and Blogs

Athletes who aspire to careers in broadcasting or other forms of media have gravitated toward podcasting. Dozens of athletes have started their own podcasts, with some going at it alone and others partnering with podcast networks like iHeart Radio. Some podcast networks are paying athletes to host podcasts, with a combination of a flat fee per episode and commission on ads placed on the show (many of which have affiliate links or codes). Athletes who produce their own podcasts can monetize with title sponsorships and ads they land on their own or through ad networks that place ads on podcasts.

Mo Hasan, a former Vanderbilt and USC quarterback, started a podcast even before the NIL rules changed, saying he was going to do it either way. Accordingly, his strategy for the *Momentum Podcast* didn't change with the NIL rules. "Regardless of ability to monetize, I always felt that things such as consistency and strategy with regard to style of content would be constant," said Hasan. "It only changed to the effect that a few podcast networks reached out to us with interest in signing with them. Typically, they asked for too much revenue and at the time I felt like it made more sense to continue building it independently."

Hasan has continued his podcast into his professional career playing for the Tennessee Titans (more on that in Chapter 10) and says it's helped connect him with numerous people and opportunities for the future. His advice for current college athletes considering starting a podcast is to make sure you fully commit to it. "The most important thing to remember when creating a podcast is consistency," he explains. "If you say you're going to post a new episode every Tuesday at 4 p.m., then it has to happen or you'll begin to lose the audience. There are thousands of other podcasts out there, therefore building that trust with your audience is critical."

Hasan says you don't need the most expensive equipment on the market to get started. Instead, just start with what you have and build from there. Not only can the podcast expose you to more people and opportunities, it also provides great social content. "A benefit of hosting a podcast is the ability to cut each episode

59

NIL Activities and Opportunities

into multiple 'micro clips' that can be posted across platforms," he says. "A one-hour conversation can lead to five to eight clips that each reach hundreds of thousands of views. In an NIL age where content and engagement is king, the ability to create this volume worth of content with only a 60-minute commitment once a week is useful."

After college, Hasan did finally sign with the Mercury podcast network. Prior to that, he said brands reached out to him directly on Instagram, over email, or through his agent. "If an athlete can sign with a podcast network on favorable terms (revenue sharing and the ability to terminate at any time), then I would go in that direction," Hasan said. "Especially if they provide services such as editing and producing."

Chloe Mitchell was on the receiving end of a podcast offer that ended up being too good to be true. "I was initially informed that I would be 'helping to launch a network,' with promises of a 'team of editors' and 'significant advertising investment' behind the show. Unfortunately, the reality was quite different. It became clear that the producers were more focused on leveraging my TikTok viewership to launch the network. Despite this, I was compensated less than $50 per episode and faced several challenges working with their team."

However, Mitchell says, she did learn from the experience. "While the experience didn't align with my expectations, it was a valuable lesson in the importance of working with people who value *me* as a person, not just what I bring to the table. It also reinforced the need to be cautious about accepting projects based on promises of exposure."

Athletes are also getting paid to make appearances on podcasts and radio shows, as opposed to hosting their own. *The JBoy Show*, an SEC-centric college football podcast hosted by former college football coach Jake "JBoy" Crain, signed seven SEC football student-athletes for weekly segments on the show during the 2021 season. Each student-athlete received $500 per show for 15 weeks, totaling $7,500 each.

Then–Auburn quarter Bo Nix was one of the athletes signed by *The Jboy Show*, but he also received weekly paychecks to appear that season on another show, *The Next Round*.

TexAgs.com, a Texas-A&M-focused media platform, paid 2021 Texas A&M football players Isaiah Spiller and Demani Richardson $10,000 each for exclusive feature interviews during SEC Media Days as part of a deal with a local company, GreenPrint Real Estate Group.[5]

Another form of content where athletes can make money is through blogging. Some athletes have already created blogs as part of their classwork, and this may be an opportunity to monetize something that also relates to their future career. One athlete I spoke with had a nutrition blog prior to NIL, and she was starting to reach out to potential sponsors to sell ads on the site. An aspiring nutritionist, she also wanted to use the blog to grow her professional portfolio prior to graduation.

Books

Other athletes who enjoy writing have turned to authoring books. One of the most successful has been Duke track and field and cross country athlete Emily Cole's sports nutrition book, *The Players' Plate: An Unorthodox Guide to Sports Nutrition*. Within just two months of its November 2022 release, it had already sold 3,500 copies and gained her multiple national media interviews (which no doubt attracted more NIL deals). By the end of 2024, Cole had sold nearly 10,000 copies.

Cole took a hybrid publishing course through the Creator Institute at Georgetown University, which allowed her to partner with an editor and publisher to bring her book to life. She ran a pre-order campaign where she offered perks to readers like getting their name in the back of the book, picking the cover, attending her launch party, participating in a Q&A, or even getting an extra recipe from her. The initial launch was so successful that Cole later recorded and released an audiobook version.

When asked what advice she'd give to other athletes wanting to write a book, Cole said to start with this question: What message or feeling do you want readers to take away? "For me, the driving force behind *The Players' Plate* was my experience with hyponatremia and a two-day coma at 17, which gave me a deep passion for teaching others about hydration and nutrition. Writing a book as a student-athlete is extremely challenging, so it must be a topic you feel compelled to share, one that feels urgent and important to you."

From there, Cole suggests you create a roadmap for your content. She says her experience with the Creator Institute was invaluable.

"It provided invaluable structure, editors at every stage, and a community of peers pursuing similar goals. This accountability helped me navigate the process from start to finish, even when I missed deadlines or faced challenges."

Don't be afraid to ask for help. Cole says she never hesitated to lean on her support system:

> *Be disciplined in your writing process, and don't hesitate to ask for help – whether from editors, mentors, or friends who can provide feedback. Doing so will only deepen the connection of your book with the people in your life – or your platforms. I personally thoroughly involved my family, friends, and followers in the process – asking for their input on the title, sharing behind-the-scenes updates, and even documenting the recording of the audiobook during my final track season at Duke. It kept me accountable and made it feel more like a team effort, so they are also excited about and inspired to share your book once it finally publishes.*

Exit 56 offers athletes another option for publication. The company began by focusing on illustrated books by football athletes that allowed the athletes to tell their own stories. The first book, *The Men Up Front*, was published in January 2022 with Michigan offensive linemen Zak Zinter, Trevor Keegan, and Ryan Hayes, who all went on to play in the NFL.

"I still remember the first sales of the book," Exit 56's CEO Andy Vodopia said. "I was in Disney World with my wife and all of a sudden my phone started blowing up. The players had posted about the book to social media, and I had my website set up to send a notification to my phone when a sale was made. I had to turn my phone off!"

At Michigan's spring game that year, the athletes were able to sign copies for fans. It was a fun moment for some of their mothers, who got to watch their sons in action.

"It was fun after the game – a few fans had their copies of the book and asked the boys to sign them at the game. We got some pics of this; the look on the fans faces' was so sweet! We thanked them for buying a book and they said, 'No, thank you – this is just so cool!'" said Keegan's mother, Amanda Keegan.

"A father bought the book for his ten-year-old son, and he read the cover and started chanting, 'The men up front, the men up front,'" said Vodopia. "He was still chanting as he walked away. I actually got a little emotional."

Penn State offensive lineman Landon Tengwall and quarterback Drew Allar were the next to publish with Exit 56, when Tengwall's *The Men Up Front* and Allar's *The Men in Back* came out. Vodopia says Allar was able to sell the first 100 signed copies in just 24 hours after posting a single tweet. Allar later announced he was donating all proceeds to charity and continued to find success selling his book.

Nebraska wide receiver Malachi Coleman was next with *Fly Like Chi!*, which details his story of being abandoned by his parents and then living in foster care with his sister until they were later adopted together. Former Huskers head coach Tom Osborne wrote the foreword for the book, and Coleman chose to donate all proceeds to care for other children in foster care.

"You hear a lot about how NIL has made a lot of athletes selfish. In my experience it's been just the opposite," said Vodopia. "Each of the athletes I've worked with has given more to charity than the books have made for themselves. So far, we've raised over $50,000 for charity between cash and book donations. So it's been a very positive experience for both the athletes and Exit 56."

The Athlete's NIL Playbook

Public Speaking and Messaging

Athletes have been asked to speak at booster clubs and other events for years, but it wasn't until the advent of NIL that they could begin earning speaking fees. From speaking at nonprofit fundraisers to Rotary clubs, corporate events, and national conferences, athletes can command fees in the thousands per speech – or, for a select few, ten thousand or more.

Riley Simmons, a women's thrower who spent time on the track and field teams at Mississippi State, Florida State, and Memphis, has wanted to be a public speaker since high school. Prior to NIL, she had experience speaking at banquets, funerals, and other opportunities like that, but she had her sights set on becoming a motivational speaker.

Once NIL began, she started looking for her first gig and reached out to her old high school coaches and told them she wanted to share her story with other athletes. Having transferred multiple times, she'd been through a lot of adversity in her sport and in life. "I came out and spoke to my old high school girls basketball team, and that was the first time I ever spoke in front of athletes. It wasn't paid or anything, I just knew that I needed to get some experience."

Simmons said it felt easiest to reach out to a coach she already knew and speak to some girls she already knew. That helped her go in confidently. Since then, she's been emailing around looking for more speaking opportunities. After relocating to Memphis, Simmons reached out to Hamilton High School in Memphis and landed a gig:

> I emailed just about every high school principal, and I would cc the athletic director, because I'm specifically trying to target athletes right now. And so I would email the principal and the athletic director, and I made myself a little flier with my picture, my email, my goals, what I do and why I want to speak.

This led to a speaking opportunity with Hamilton High School in Memphis to speak to all of their female athletes. "It's really about just taking a leap of faith and sending as many emails as you can." She's also working her connections and says that's helped open doors with other high schools when people are willing to reach out to their alma maters on her behalf.

Simmons has also been paid to speak as part of a community service project. She's started fielding some requests for speaking and is trying to decide how to price herself going forward. She credits Sam Green, known as the "Athletes' Go-To Content Creator," with the best advice she's received on pricing herself. "She told me, 'If you get too many yesses, you're too cheap. If you get too many noes, you're too expensive. When you're getting the same amount of yesses and noes, you know you're priced just right.'"

Dorie Clark, a keynote speaker who interviewed other speakers for her book, *Entrepreneurial You*, says speaking for free in the beginning is a reasonable strategy to build your skills. She also points out that even unpaid speaking often gets you paid travel to fun places to visit when events are held in other locations. Those early free gigs are also a good way to get video clips to create a reel and ask organizers for recommendations you can use on your website, social media, and other marketing.

You may also decide you are willing to speak for free to nonprofit organizations you have a connection with. or in front of audiences that are of particular importance to you, or where you have an opportunity to sell something, like a book you've written. Don't mistake this with not *deserving* to get paid, though. These are exceptions you make because they serve another goal or mission.

So what happens when you've got a few speaking engagements under your belt and are ready to get paid? Clark suggests asking about their budget.[6] I second this advice, as they may say a number

66

The Athlete's NIL Playbook

even higher than you were planning, so it keeps you from underpricing yourself.

Don't overthink how to say it. You can ask something as simple as "What's your budget for a speaker?" They'll generally offer a flat fee plus travel expenses.

If, however, they ask about your fee, I'm sorry to say there's not a one-size-fits-all way to determine this. Much like you'll find with social media marketing, there are online calculators that can help you determine a fee based on factors such as the number of speaking engagements you've had, the expected number in attendance, and the like. However, these don't take into account unique aspects about you or your talk, so they should be only a part of your process.

Some people determine their fee by setting a per-person number. Others use an hourly rate, taking into account the amount of time they'll be traveling to and from the event, in addition to the speech itself. Speakers might also add on to that amount if they'll need to customize their speech and/or slides for that particular audience.

Dozens of professional speakers have written on the subject of pricing. Reviewing their advice indicates a range of suggested starting fees of $500 to $2,500. That's a pretty big range, but it gives you a starting point.

I'd take into account whom you're speaking in front of. For example, if a high school asks you to come speak to their athletes, you'd probably be on the lower end of that scale. If it's a large conference where attendees are paying to attend, however, you could probably ask for the higher end. If you have to travel to speak, you should also be getting your travel expenses covered.

As you gain more experience, you can increase your fees. Once you have someone answer the budget question, that might also give you an idea of where you should be at. Those who are speaking on a regular basis but don't have a household name or multiple books

NIL Activities and Opportunities

or other recognized credentials will likely be in the $5,000–$10,000 range. If you're well known in your niche – or on the field, court, track, and so on – you might be able to command $20,000 or more.

Also, note that you can get paid for virtual speaking as well. I generally charge about one-third of my normal speaking fee for a virtual engagement. And as is the case with in-person events, I do take on some for free if it's for another business purpose (such as supporting professors who use my books in their classrooms) or to support a mission or charity for which I advocate.

Although the dollar amounts might be lower, athletes can also earn money by filming messages for fans on platforms like Cameo. Athletes record birthday messages, pep talks, advice, and more, setting their own fees for creating the content.

In the first few months of NIL in 2021, more than 350 college athletes across almost every sport and division joined Cameo. Remember that myth about how NIL is only for male athletes? Then–Alabama softball athlete Montana Fouts was the top earner on the platform in the first few months by a landslide.

Texas volleyball athlete Emma Halter said she joined Cameo in 2023 and had completed approximately 80 videos by early 2025. Her personalized videos start at $30 and allow customers to get anything from a birthday shout-out to volleyball tips. "I love how I know I am bringing joy into someone else's life by making Cameos," said Halter.

The time commitment is low, she says. "You just have to keep your eye out for requests. It takes only a few minutes."

She does see a spike in sales during her own season but also around nationals for club volleyball season when people are asking for good-luck videos for teams or players.

Halter drives traffic to her Cameo through Instagram stories and her Instagram bio, but people also simply find her on Cameo. "I think Cameo can be right for anyone who likes to interact with their audience/fans. I also love to help young athletes, and Cameo is a great place to give athletes tips for their sport in a short video."

Music

Another off-the-field hobby – or professional pursuit – athletes are now monetizing is their music. Although athletes could acquire waivers prior to NIL to allow them to monetize things such as music, they couldn't use their position as a college athlete to promote their products or events or use it as the basis of the product or service.

That's why former Marshall offensive lineman Will Ulmer was using the stage name "Lucky Bill" prior to NIL. A country music singer and songwriter, Ulmer released a new single on the first day of changed NIL rules.

"Music is something I'm really passionate about and it's not something I've been able to fairly pursue, I feel like," Ulmer told the *Herald-Dispatch*. "I just think this is big because it gives me an opportunity to use my name and my likeness to do something that I love and enjoy doing."[7]

Rapper Flau'jae Johnson, a women's basketball player at LSU, has a huge following that loves both her basketball and her music content. She's been able to land multiple NIL deals, including being the first athlete to sign with JBL.

Johnson can even add "Super Bowl commercial" to her résumé. She was hired by Louisiana-based Gordon McKernan Injury Attorneys to remix the company's jingle during the Super Bowl in 2024.[8]

Art

When NIL began, the very first athlete to reach out to me was Wichita State softball athlete Syd McKinney. She wanted advice on her brand,

and the first thing I noticed was that she had an Etsy link in her Instagram bio but no images of artwork in her feed, only softball photos.

McKinney was adding custom artwork to sneakers when she first started her Etsy store, but as her brand blossomed with NIL, so did her artwork. First, she added paintings on canvas, and then she landed an incredible NIL deal with HomeGrown, a chain of breakfast/brunch restaurants in the Midwest. They were looking for a local artist to help decorate a new location and having worked with McKinney on a commercial in 2021, they remembered seeing her art on her Instagram.

Syd is just one of many athletes now pursuing their passion for art and monetizing it thanks to NIL. Ra-Sun Kazadi was playing football for SMU when NIL restrictions were removed in 2021. He wasn't the star player or a household name, playing in just 10 games over two seasons with a couple of tackles in his stat line.

Ra-Sun the artist, however, is thriving after getting a jump start with NIL. His first internship came from an SMU alum, which ended up leading to a commission from the Kansas City Royals Foundation in honor of their 2014 ALCS Championship. That experience led him to working with the Dallas Mavericks and Carolina Panthers.

"All those are things that I can directly say trace back to NIL," he said. He explains that he wasn't as motivated to work on his art prior to NIL because of the hoops you had to jump through in order to make money on outside endeavors.

"The rule change in NIL helped me as an artist because I could actually promote my work, put my name to my work, show up at shows, and be able to sell my work."

Like Ulmer, Kazadi was working on his passion without attaching his name to it prior to NIL, unable to have shows or promote his work on his social media. "It was just basically relying on people to know that I was an artist and then doing stuff for super cheap," Kazadi told ESPN in 2022.[9] Although he once felt lucky to make $30 for a sketch or $100 for a painting, NIL allowed him to promote his work on a broader scale, significantly increasing his rates.

But for him it was about more than just the money. "I'm able to grow as an artist and then explore other stuff," he said. "If I'm like, 'Oh, it'd be cool to paint on some pants, or be cool to paint on a T-shirt,' I can explore different executions. I can do a mural because now I'm not like, 'Oh, wow, I only have $300 for food, gas, and everything for this month. Let me try and go get a painting [done for money] real quick.' So it's good."

Today, Kazadi has moved out of the locker room and into an art studio, pursuing his art full time as an artist and graphic designer.

His advice to athletes with artistic aspirations coming up behind him is to start early. "My advice to high school students or college students behind me is just start now. Start as soon as you can, make a lot of mistakes, and learn from them."

NIL Activities and Opportunities

He also suggested finding mentors early on and giving yourself space to experiment. "Like for me, being a creative, I looked at it as not just being an artist. Look at what you could do with design. Look at what you could do with art. Look at what you could do with being a creative strategist or working with companies."

Car Deals and Other Free Products and Services

Not all NIL deals will be for cash. Many will be for free products or services, from a $27 tube of mascara to massage guns, mattresses, and even cars.

Athletes should weigh the market value of the product or service against what they would normally charge for the promotion being asked for by the brand. A tube of mascara might not be worth the time it takes to create two Instagram feed posts and a story, but cryotherapy once a week for a month might be.

The valuation will vary from one student to the next, but it's essential that athletes know their value and negotiate to get it even in free product deals.

Car Deals

Athletes were rumored to be receiving cars under the table long before NIL, so it's no surprise they were some of the flashiest and most newsworthy deals when the rules changed.

The first car deal made public was for then–LSU quarterback Myles Brennan with Hollingsworth Richards Ford for an F-250. Within days of the deal being announced, Brennan broke his arm during a freak fishing accident.

Because NIL deals can't be based on athletic performance under NCAA rules, the dealership wouldn't have been able to end the deal simply because Brennan wasn't playing, but it did expose the risk dealerships were taking with these deals if they were counting on backing an athlete at the beginning of the season on the assumption they'd be in the spotlight. Unfortunately, the injury was the end of Brennan's football career.[10]

The vast majority of car deals are short-term leases that last the season, six months, or perhaps a year. It's important to note that the athlete will be issued a 1099 for the fair market value of the lease, which the athlete will need to report on their taxes. The athlete is responsible for insurance on the vehicle as well, unless other arrangements have been made as part of the deal.

Although most car deals are individual arrangements between dealerships and athletes, the Crimson Collective, which supports University of Utah athletes, did team-wide car deals for athletes on Utah's football, men's and women's basketball, and women's gymnastics teams. The initial leases were six months and insurance was also covered by the collective. In exchange, the athletes committed to promoting the collective.[11]

You'll find most athletes doing social media promotion as part of these car deals, with some also combining personal appearances and autograph signings at the dealership.

Medical Services

Athletes have been landing NIL deals for services such as massage, cryotherapy, teeth whitening, and more. One of the more interesting ones, however, is Howard men's basketball athletes receiving free eye care, including SMILE surgery.

Dr. Bruce Rivers, an alumnus of Howard University College of Medicine, reached out to Daniel Marks, the chief program strategist for Howard men's basketball, because he wanted to offer the athletes free SMILE surgery. The SMILE procedure is similar to LASIK eye surgery, but more advanced and with a much shorter recovery time.

Through his eye practice, Envue Eye Center, Dr. Rivers provided free eye exams to the entire 2023–2024 team. Four players were eligible for the SMILE surgery and received it in the summer of 2023: Reece Brown, Aaron Roberson, Shy Odum, and Isiah Warfield. In 2025, freshman Calvin Robins Jr. was scheduled to have the surgery as well.

"Isiah was a unique case as he was a player with terrible vision, who refused to wear contacts and would not wear prescription goggles, so for his first three college seasons, he was basically playing games with severely limited vision," said Marks. "[In 2023–2024], he saw marked improvement in his 3P shooting (+6.9%) and FT shooting (+11.9%) after the procedure."

Marks says Coach Blakeney valued Dr. Rivers's contributions so much that he was awarded a MEAC Championship ring alongside the team.

Real Estate Training

Although much of the news coverage around NIL focuses on flashy deals and checks with a lot of zeros, the true lasting impact is in how it can impact an athlete beyond graduation and well past their playing days.

One of the biggest programs launched to date focused on future career paths for athletes is NIL Real Estate, a division of Keller Williams. What began as a pilot program at BYU to assist athletes in getting their real estate license is now available to athletes nationwide.

In 2022, more than 120 athletes signed up for the program, which gave them access to 120 hours of on-demand video education required to earn their real estate license in Utah. When completed, the athletes were prepared to take both the state and national exams required to obtain their licenses.

Without the program, athletes would have typically spent $650–$1,000 for a real estate education course, plus an additional $250–$500 for a test prep service. Participants in the program who pass their exam also have their monthly agent fees to Keller Williams absorbed by NIL Real Estate.

Of the 120 student-athletes who signed up for the BYU program in 2022, 36 had completed their courses as of May 2023, with 10 having already taken and passed their exams. Five student-athletes had referred buyers or sellers to Keller Williams and earned referral commission.

One BYU men's tennis athlete earned his license and then bought a starter home for himself and his wife. The Keller Williams team loved the story so much that he was awarded 65% of the commission rather than the customary 35%, which resulted in him pocketing $6,300 in commission on the purchase of his home.

In May 2023, NIL Real Estate expanded the program across the country, opening it to all college athletes. As of August 2024, 804 athletes from 202 schools had signed up and were at various stages of the education program or test prep. Seventeen former college athletes who completed the program were working full-time in real estate, and another eight had their referral license.

Thanks to NIL, these athletes are leaving school with not only a degree but also a real estate license and the ability to start working and earning immediately after graduation.

■ ■ ■

It's important to note that athletes are still responsible for taxes on the value of any free product, services, leases, and even travel provided by brands. If the value is more than $600, you should expect to receive a Form 1099 from the brand. You should closely track everything you receive to ensure you're abiding by applicable tax laws and reporting these correctly.

It would be impossible to cover every type of NIL, because the opportunities are virtually limitless. The rest of the book, however, will attempt to highlight some of the most prominent types of deals, the process for landing them (including real-life examples and templates!), and how to protect both yourself and your intellectual property.

Key Takeaways

- NIL opportunities extend far beyond social media posts and include lessons/camps, merchandise, podcasting, books, appearances, artwork, music, and more. Athletes should explore options that align with their interests and skills.
- Athletes at all levels and with modest social media followings can secure valuable NIL deals. Many brands value authenticity, engagement, and the connection to specific communities over raw follower counts.
- All sponsored content must include clear disclosures in accordance with Federal Trade Commission guidelines.
- Many NIL opportunities provide value through free products, services, career development, or business experiences that can be beneficial long after athletic careers end.
- Athletes are responsible for taxes on all NIL income, including the value of free products, services, leases, and travel. Tracking all compensation is essential for proper tax reporting.
- Each NIL opportunity should be evaluated not just for immediate compensation but for how it contributes to building your overall personal brand and future opportunities.

Chapter 3

Defining and Growing Your Personal Brand

Although I know some of you reading this are parents, I'm going to talk directly to your athletes in the next few chapters.

"Personal brand" is one of those buzzwords that gets used a lot, but that no one really understands. What is a personal brand?

Boiled down to its essence, your personal brand is what other people think about you.

That's the thing about a personal brand. Although it's intensely personal, it's also not something completely within your control. Don't worry, though, we're going to talk about how you can intentionally shape it to reflect you, your values, and your passions. And also how that's going to help you attract more NIL opportunities. Just as no two personal brands are the same, there are also no two ways to leverage and monetize your NIL.

Developing Your NIL Strategy: The Three Questions

I'm all about approaching NIL in a strategic way, because there's a lot more you can do with it than simply making $100 on an Instagram post. Whether it's a long-term contract that pays you consistently or a deal that opens the door to your future post-graduation, NIL can be so much more.

There's no one-size-fits-all strategy for NIL. Instead, I want to give you a playbook that allows you to select the right play for your individual situation. When I speak with college and high school athletes, I start by asking them to answer three questions:

- What do you already enjoy doing outside of your sport?
- What do you want to do after graduation?
- What are one to three things you want to be known for?

What Do You Already Enjoy Doing Outside of Your Sport?

I start with this question because the easiest – and most fun – way to make money is doing something you already enjoy doing. For example, if you have fun posting your #OOTD (outfit of the day) on Instagram, then partnering with brands and boutiques to create more Instagram content is a great idea. Maybe an affiliate program such as LIKEtoKNOW.it would be a good fit.

However, if you haven't posted on Instagram in three months, and creating content on the platform feels like a chore, you probably shouldn't try to monetize there just because it's what you see other athletes doing.

Instead, maybe you love working with youth athletes. Platforms like Coach Tube will help you monetize lessons and recorded trainings. Or you might be an artist or musician like Syd McKinney or Will Ulmer (mentioned in the previous chapter), in which case you should concentrate your NIL efforts there.

The key is to lean into something you're already doing instead of creating more work for yourself. Not only will you be more likely to have the time necessary to monetize it, but you're less likely to get burned out or frustrated.

What Do You Want to Do After Graduation?

One of the smartest things an athlete can do with NIL is use it to engage with people, companies, and deals that help them get to where they want to be after graduation.

"The NIL has opened the door for student athletes to leverage their school's platform to begin building their personal brand, a personal brand that will follow a student-athlete long after graduation," said Caroline Frazier, a former dual-sport athlete turned broadcaster who helps athletes with personal branding. "The four to five years of college can catapult even the most average athlete into stardom with the right combination of a willingness to share, a little business savvy, and a vulnerability that can connect beyond sports."

For example, I know athletes who are asking for sit-downs with key executives at companies as part of their NIL deal to promote the company on social media. They're getting facetime and networking with people they might want to work for down the road.

I know athletes who are forming LLCs and getting real-world experience running their own company, doing things like creating business plans, marketing strategies, and more. They're learning how to create products and find manufacturers and distributors.

In the introduction, you heard about how Anna Camden used NIL to set herself up for a career in broadcasting after graduation and how Leah Clapper leveraged the skills she gained through NIL to land her first full-time job after graduation.

During her last summer at the University of Florida, Clapper got connected with a venture capital company in San Francisco to help manage their social media on a contract basis. When she graduated, they brought her on full-time to run their social media and produce a podcast. Within a year, she was leading content strategy and running other content initiatives for the brand, achieving 13 times growth for the podcast in her first year.

"I wouldn't have landed where I am today if it weren't for NIL and the invaluable lessons I learned about social media through that experience," Clapper said.

We'll dive more into leveraging NIL beyond graduation in Chapter 10.

What Are One to Three Things You Want to Be Known For?

I previously owned a public relations agency that focused on representing solopreneurs, and this is an exercise I went through with every client. I'd go so far as to say it's the most important building block when it comes to leveraging your own NIL for opportunities. Not only does it attract people and brands, it attracts the *right* people and brands.

Remember when we started the chapter off with the idea that your personal brand is simply what other people think of when they hear your name? In my NIL classes, I partner students up, and I have them look at each other's social media, websites, LinkedIn profiles, and other publicly available information. Then I have them tell the person what they think their brand is based on what they found.

About 50% of the time, the person being reviewed says their brand was at least partially accurate, but 50% of the time, they say it's not at all what they want to be known for. That's okay, because you can intentionally craft your personal brand, and this is my favorite exercise for doing so.

I call this the three bucket exercise. Each of the three buckets represents one thing you want to be known for. The first time I gave this exercise to a PR client, I didn't give a limit and the client came back with 10 buckets. The problem with having that many is that people will be confused. They'll have no idea who you really are.

From a PR perspective – and this applies to NIL – it makes it tough for a brand to understand if you're aligned and if you can help them get in front of the right audience.

As entrepreneur and best-selling author Seth Godin reminds us, "When you speak to everyone, you speak to no one."

For the purposes of this exercise, your three things should be hobbies or skills. The first time I did this exercise in an NIL class, the responses were characteristics like being loyal, trustworthy, or dedicated. While all those things are valuable, they're not what we're looking for here.

As an example, here are the three things I want to be known for.

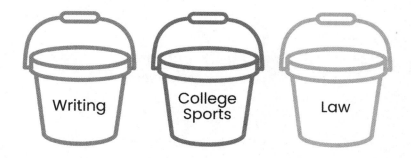

Whenever I do something forward-facing – a blog post, speech, interview, social media post, or the like – I want it to fit in one of those three buckets. By concentrating on the things I do in the public eye, I can help guide people's perception of my brand toward what I want it to be.

Not only does it allow the right audience and partners to find me, it also makes it easier for me to say no to opportunities that aren't a fit. When I get asked to do something professionally, I ask myself if it fits in one of my three buckets. If it doesn't, I say no.

For example, I still get asked to speak on PR topics because I previously owned a PR agency. Recently, I got asked to speak on a

Defining and Growing Your Personal Brand

podcast about how entrepreneurs can get themselves interviewed on more television shows. That's something I've written and spoken on many times in the past, so I *could* do it. However, it's no longer something I want to be known for, so I should say no. This frees up my time so I can say yes to something that's a better fit. That way if I get asked next week to do a podcast interview at the same time on how college athletes can monetize their NIL, I have the time to do that interview, which aligns more with my current brand.

As you see with my example, however, your brand isn't static. It can fluctuate, and many of you will experience that as you leave your sport, whether that's immediately after college or after a professional sports career. Right now, your sport is probably one of those buckets. It might even be after you stop playing if you become a broadcaster or coach in your sport. However, if you become an accountant and your sport is no longer part of your everyday life, that bucket might change to finance/accounting.

Law was one of my buckets when I was a practicing lawyer, and even into my becoming a sports business reporter, but then I dropped it when I was running my PR agency, and now it's back since I returned to reporting.

Michael Raymond, an agent with a law degree who is certified by the NBPA (National Basketball Players Association), has been representing college athletes since the beginning of NIL. His agency, Raymond Representation, has worked with more than 50 athletes and closed more than 1,000 deals in the first three years of NIL, collaborating with more than 500 brands.

Raymond says it's imperative for both success in college and after graduation to showcase your hobbies outside of your sport. "Emily Cole is the perfect example. She talks about health and fitness, she features content with her sister (who is a country music singer) where they're singing in the car and showcasing new songs, and she shows running different trails around different states."

As she transitioned out of college in 2024, her content shifted from running at Duke to running trails as a hobby. Raymond represents Cole and says her content has attracted many different brand deals because they can see a way to be featured inside of her existing content, so her audience doesn't feel like it's just being sold to. "You can't connect with brands if you're just posting content from your sport," Raymond advises.

So, back to your three buckets. Your sport might be an easy bucket, but what are your other two? I'd say at least one should be your favorite hobby: fashion, fishing, hunting, painting, singing – anything you enjoy outside of your sport. You could even have two of your buckets be hobbies.

Maybe you have a dog who is a loyal companion, and you take him on all your adventures. Then he might be a bucket! One of the first NIL deals reported on July 1, 2021, was for Arkansas wide receiver Trey Knox and his dog, Blue, with PetSmart.

A bucket could also relate to your future career ambitions, such as "Kids" if you want to work with children, or "Speaking" if you want to become a motivational speaker.

Frazier agrees with my three-topic strategy and challenges athletes to post solely about those three topics for 30 days. Here are her suggestions for content:

- **Sport:** Post reels focused around "day in the life" content of a game day, practice days, travel days, and the like. Tag your team's account, university's account, and any place you visit during the day that has a social media presence. Don't stop with just one reel! Focus on creating one or two a week for 30 days.

- **Hobby:** Create carousel posts with things you enjoyed from the week: yoga class, sitting on campus on a beautiful day, favorite lunch spot. There's one catch: nothing from your sport.

83

Defining and Growing Your Personal Brand

These are all things outside of your sport that make you *you*! Focus on posting a carousel of hobbies outside of your sport once a week.

- **Dream:** What's next for you? Sharing your dreams with your audience will only open doors and opportunity. You will build an audience who is rooting for you and will celebrate your success outside of sports just as they did in your sport. Focus on posting one or two stories a week on what you want your next chapter of life to look like.

"By the end of this 3/30 approach, a student athlete will have begun their personal branding journey," Frazier explains. "They can pull analytics to see growth and engagement and start learning their new audience. A student-athlete's personal social media page has now become their business plan, and the NIL has made them legitimate entrepreneurs with an eager audience."

Take a little time before moving on to the next section and come up with your three buckets.

You are what other people see and hear, so send a clear message.

The Riches Are in the Niches

It's a common misconception that the sheer volume of your audience will determine your NIL opportunities or compensation. That may be truer for some kinds of NIL, such as public appearances or autograph signings. Name recognition and the size of the interested audience may be the sole factors in those decisions.

However, when we get into social media marketing, brands are generally looking to reach a specific audience, not just anyone. Multiple studies have shown that it's actually micro-influencers (15,000–75,000 followers) and nano-influencers (fewer than 15,000 followers) who have the highest engagement rates on social media.

For example, if a company that makes hiking boots wants to work with an athlete, they'd likely be better off working with someone with 10,000 followers who regularly creates hiking content and gets engagement from their audience than with someone whose has 100,000 followers but has never posted hiking content.

Your sport is a niche you're already in, and you'll likely find brands within your sport interested in working with athletes. But it's also important to showcase your interests outside of your sport, which can offer additional opportunities and provide continued work even beyond your days as an athlete.

"Sports can get you noticed, but it is what you share outside of sports that makes you unforgettable." That's what Blake Lawrence, the CEO of athlete influencer platform Opendorse, said when I asked him how important it is for athletes to develop a niche. "Every athlete has passions beyond the game," he continued. "It is just a matter of showing them to the world. That is where meaningful connections with followers happen, and that is what leads to brand partnerships that truly resonate."

In Chapter 10, we're going to talk more about how you can take NIL beyond college graduation, but it all starts with developing content outside of your sport. In addition to giving you that longevity, it can also attract more brand deals.

"Brands do not just partner with athletes." Lawrence said. "They partner with personalities. They filter first by sport, but they are ultimately looking for athletes who align with their niche. Sharing your interests and passions outside of sports is the fastest way to stand out and show brands why you are the perfect fit."

Art, music, fashion, hunting, fishing – these are all areas where athletes have created niches that attracted brand partners.

On July 12, 2021, Arkansas wide receiver Treylon Burks posted an image on Instagram of a bed covered in gear from a hunting brand, Banded. In the photo, you can see multiple backpacks, hats,

85

Defining and Growing Your Personal Brand

shirts, and more. Even two years later as an NFL player, Burks was still posting hunting content on his Instagram.

Former Alabama softball player Montana Fouts also shared her hunting hobby on her social media. In August 2022, she announced a deal with Summit Stands, which sells tree stands and other hunting gear. She also partnered with Boombah for a co-branded line of clothing and gear, including camo prints on hoodies and bat bags.

The 2024 Heisman Trophy winner, Travis Hunter, has multiple deals related to one of his favorite hobbies outside of football: fishing. He often features fishing on his YouTube channel, which has nearly 500,000 subscribers as of this writing. He's worked with brands such as WaterLand Co, Gary Yamamoto Custom Baits, and KastKing.

As mentioned earlier in this chapter, you might even find NIL success by focusing some of your content on man's best friend. Trey Knox's deal with PetSmart wasn't the only NIL action we've seen for athletes and their canine companions. South Carolina wide receiver Antwane Wells Jr.'s dog, Sosa, helped him land an NIL partnership with the Farmer's Dog, a dog food brand. Texas Tech quarterback Tyler Shough's golden retriever, Murphy, helped him sign a deal with Wagbnb, a high-end hotel, daycare, and spa for dogs and cats.

Collectives have even gotten in on the action. The Massachusetts Collective partnered with former UMass women's basketball player Sam Breen's dog, Turbo, to create a new line of treats.[1]

Showcasing your hobbies and interests outside of your sport is paramount to continuing NIL activities after your days as a college athlete, especially within social media marketing. We'll discuss more about building a brand that takes you beyond graduation in Chapter 10, but also keep in mind that it's never too early to start building your brand, either. This book highlights several youth and high school athletes who've been able to take advantage of NIL opportunities, and starting younger gives brands a longer runway to work with you.

Key Takeaways

- Your personal brand is ultimately what other people think about you. While not entirely within your control, you can intentionally shape how you're perceived through strategic content creation and messaging.
- Focus on three areas or "buckets" you want to be known for, which usually includes your sport plus two other hobbies or interests. This helps you build an audience that is valuable to brands in those spaces.
- Your athletic career will eventually end, but a well-developed personal brand can continue generating opportunities long after. Developing content outside your sport ensures brand sustainability.
- The easiest and most sustainable NIL opportunities come from monetizing activities you already enjoy. Don't create extra work by forcing yourself into areas that don't interest you naturally.
- Brands often value engaged, targeted audiences over sheer follower count. Micro-influencers (15,000-75,000 followers) and nano-influencers (under 15,000 followers) frequently have higher engagement rates than mega-influencers.
- It's never too early to begin building your personal brand. Starting younger gives brands a longer runway to work with you and helps establish your identity beyond your athletic achievements.

Defining and Growing Your Personal Brand

Chapter 4

Social Media Marketing

In the second year of NIL (2022–2023), compliance software INFLCR reported that 70% of all NIL transactions reported through their platform were for social media and royalty payouts.

Competitor Opendorse reported 57.95% of all commercial NIL deals on their platform were for social media posts. Although both companies saw decreases when they issued their 2023–2024 reports, social media marketing remains one of the most accessible avenues for NIL monetization for athletes.

Authors of an article in *Harvard Business Review* in 2024 found that even top brands didn't focus solely on athletes with the largest followings. "Only 29% had more than 100,000 followers. In fact, 59% had fewer than 50,000 followers, 14% had from 2,000 to 5,000, and 3% had fewer than 2,000."

They also found 50% of sponsored athletes came from sports other than football or men's basketball.[1] In Opendorse's 2024 report on the third year of NIL, the company found women's volleyball athletes had seen the greatest number of commercial NIL deals per year since NIL began in 2021, followed by football, men's basketball, women's basketball, softball, and baseball.[2]

It doesn't matter whether you have 500 followers or 100,000 followers – you can land opportunities in this space that could include free food, fun products, and what I know you really want: cold, hard cash.

I'm probably not telling you anything you don't know, because social media NIL deals dominate the headlines. So let's dig into what you may not know.

Optimizing Your Profile

Remember how we talked in the last chapter about a personal brand being what other people think it is? That perception of your brand starts with the moment they land on your profile, which makes your profile extremely valuable real estate.

Just like you might paint the exterior of a home and add plants and flowers to give it more "curb appeal," you should also spend some time on your profile before you start reaching out to brands or joining NIL marketplaces (more on these below, but they're platforms where NIL deals are posted by brands and athletes can maintain profiles for brands to find).

Although every social media platform is a bit different, most have common features: your name, a profile photo, a short bio, and at least one link to another site.

Choosing the Right Username

Let's start with your name. For most people, using your real name is going to be your best bet so it's easy for people to find you and know they ended up in the right place. But what if you have a common name like Emily Smith? Then you might try a nickname like EmSmith or maybe add your sport or jersey number (if applicable to your sport) to make it ESmithHoops or EmilySmith5.

Another way to go is to use a nickname that's unrelated to your legal name, and that's the way I went. When I joined Twitter in 2009, most people were using catchy names that described something about their job, hobby, or interests.

When I thought about my personal brand, I thought I could stand out in the marketplace by emphasizing the fact that I was one of just a few women writing or speaking on sports business. That's how @SportsBizMiss was born, and I've used that name on every platform since.

There's a downside to using a name like SportsBizMiss, however. I often find myself at conferences in conversations with people, and 10 minutes in they finally realize that Kristi Dosh and SportsBizMiss are the same person. It's not uncommon for them to see my real name on my nametag and have no idea I'm the SportsBizMiss they follow on social media. So keep that in mind if you want to use a nickname or other catchy handle.

If you do use a nickname for your username, make sure you use your full name in the name field so you still come up in search results when a brand is looking for you.

The key is to make it easy for a brand to find you. Let's say a brand saw a news article about you, and they're convinced you're a great fit for their brand and want to reach out. Most aren't going to spend 20 minutes hunting down your profile, and you don't want them to be frustrated as they click through dozens of options trying to figure out which one is you.

Choosing the Right Profile Photo

This brings me to your profile photo. When brands are trying to find someone on social media, they're going to use a combination of your username, photo, and bio to verify they've found the right person. I strongly suggest using a photo that clearly shows your face. Choosing a photo in your uniform or other school gear might help someone confirm they've found you, but you might also choose to showcase some other aspect of your personal brand here.

Writing the Perfect Bio

Finally, you're going to bring it all home with a killer bio. In this small space, you want to showcase that personal brand we talked about in the last chapter. What are those three things you want people to take away about you when they glance at your profile? It might be your sport, your faith, and your love of fashion. Or maybe your channel is mostly about your dog and your DIY projects, with a few sports photos thrown in.

A brand might only give your profile a few seconds' glance, so ask yourself if that snapshot tells them who you are and the types of people you might help them reach. If the answer to both questions is yes, you're ready to move on to the next step.

A perfect example is Duke track and field and cross country athlete Emily Cole's profile while she was an active college athlete. At a quick glance, I know that she's a Duke athlete who authored a book (which I can click through and learn is about nutrition) and loves "running, salty water & braid buns." I could also safely assume she's proud to be from Texas.

568 posts   198K followers   677 following

EMCO
🅰 emilycole
Athlete
Texas girl who wrote a book for you @theplayersplate sharing my love for running, salty water, & braid buns 🌊
NIL: miggie@raymondrep.com
🔗 www.amazon.com/gp/aw/d/B0BLM9NZLN/ref=tmm_hrd_swatch_0?ie=UTF8 + 3

Really, I know a lot about her from a very small space. If I have a brand that's at all related to running, nutrition, hydration, or haircare, I probably feel pretty sure I've found a good candidate for a partnership, especially after I look through her content and see it matches her bio.

You might have also noticed her link goes to Amazon. That takes you to Cole's nutrition book, but what should your link go to? It could be a personal website, your profile page on a marketplace or agent's website, your Etsy site, or even to a bio tool like Linktree that allows you to showcase multiple links. Another option is to share an affiliate link or brand link here, but we'll talk more about how to price this if you're going to give it up to a brand.

Before we leave the issue of your profile, I want to say one last thing. Be consistent with your username and photo across social media platforms. Not only will this help people know they've found the right person, but it'll make life so much easier when you do something like a podcast interview and are asked to share your social handles. No one is going to remember three different usernames they hear you say, but they can probably remember one.

Level Up Your Social Media Profile: Do's and Don'ts

Profile Element	Do's	Don'ts
Username	• Use your real name when possible • Add sport/number for common names (ESmithHoops, JonesBball23) • Stay consistent across all platforms	• Pick usernames impossible to connect to you • Use different handles on different platforms • Create complicated or forgettable usernames
Profile Photo	• Show your face clearly • Consider uniform/gear shots for recognition • Choose pics that match your brand	• Use group photos where you're hard to spot • Use abstract images or random graphics

(continued)

93

Social Media Marketing

(continued)

Profile Element	Do's	Don'ts
Bio	• Clearly identify your sport and school • Highlight two or three interests/hobbies outside of your sport	• Use abbreviations that not everyone will understand • List too many random interests • Leave it empty or unfinished
Links	• Link to your website, marketplace profile, Linktree, etc.	• Link to brands, unless they've paid you for it (this is valuable real estate) • Overload with too many options
Overall Strategy	• Keep everything consistent across platforms • Make it easy for brands to find you • Update regularly as you grow	• Make brands work to confirm it's really you • Use offensive language • Set up your profile and then forget about it

Okay, now that we've got your profile putting your best foot forward, let's talk about how to get people following and engaging with you.

How to Grow Your Following and Engagement

You might think only athletes with tens of thousands or hundreds of thousands of followers land social media deals, but that couldn't be further from the truth. Brands are much more interested in what your personal brand represents, who your audience is, and how engaged they are with your content.

Being Strategic About Your Social Content

Later in this chapter, I'm going to give you a list full of ideas for content for those days when you're feeling uninspired. First, though, let's talk about the type of content that increases your engagement and grows your followers beyond doing a full content franchise like Laney Higgins and Fran Belibi (discussed below).

Sam Green, an NIL educator who brands herself as the "Athletes' Go-To Content Creator," works with athletes across the country to grow their audiences. She advises athletes to build out a two-prong approach:

- **Algorithm-based content:** This content is created with virality in mind. This usually involves a song or sound that is going viral on social media already and creating a photo or video with text on screen that's relatable about life as an athlete.

- **Brand-building content:** This is content that helps you achieve your post-college goals. Remember when we talked in the last chapter about your future objectives being part of your NIL strategy? This is content that relates to those plans.

Green said one athlete she worked with wanted to be a motivational speaker, so she helped her set up a speaking engagement at a local high school and record it to use on social media. While there's still a chance that content might go viral, Green says it's really about providing value to your audience and creating content other brands can support.

"For example, with this athlete speaking to the younger generation, she used a microphone, which could now be used to pitch to microphone companies for sponsorship of the segment," she said. "Brand-building content provides value for your own personal brand and offers opportunities for other brands to get involved."

In addition to the strategy discussed above, there are other elements you should take into account before posting on social media:

- Photos and videos should be good quality, meaning they're well-lit and not blurry or hard to hear (for video). Most smartphones have great cameras these days, so you don't need to invest in a bunch of professional equipment.

- Use hashtags related to both your messaging and the people, products, and objects in your image/video. Use a mix of more popular hashtags and smaller, more niche hashtags for the best results. Instagram allows up to 30, while other networks only have character limits for your full caption. Some people feel strongly about how many you use, but the truth is that no social media network reveals the details of its algorithm, so you have to experiment a little and see what works best for you and your audience.

- Adding your location to the post can help locals or people researching the area to find your content, although you may want to wait until you've left a location to post it, for safety reasons.

- For photos, you should also add alt text (on some platforms it's hidden in advanced settings on the post). This text is what would be read out loud to someone who is vision impaired and can't see your image, so it should describe in detail what's in the image so they can picture it. Keywords in this description can also help people find your post.

Perhaps the most important thing you can do, however, is to experiment with different types of content to find what people respond to. Some people are going to gain a following because they do funny things. Others are going to amass a following because their dog does incredible tricks. You probably follow more than one person who inspires you or whose fashion sense you admire.

Think back to those three things you want to be known for that we talked about in Chapter 3. Generally speaking, each piece of content you share should fit in one of those three buckets. The audience who is attracted to those topics might respond to different types of posts than another person's audience, so it really does take some trial and error. See a post take off? Create more like that. It really is that simple.

Also, don't forget that you're supposed to be social on social media. Engage with other accounts in your topic areas by commenting on their posts. Tag people and brands in your posts when they're part of your message or photo/video.

Becca Wathen, a former DI women's basketball athlete and current strategic partner manager for athletes at Meta, gave this advice for Instagram:

> To find success on social media, athletes should be authentic (share content that naturally represents your brand), consistent (aim to post 2-3x/week), and engaging (respond to comments, utilize engagement stickers in stories, and create content that's unique and creative). Athletes who share behind-the-scenes content and give their audience an inside look into their life, passions, and story can build an engaged and loyal audience, while simultaneously attracting brand partners.

You shouldn't be afraid to collaborate with others, either. In the next section, you'll see how previously mentioned DIII volleyball athlete Laney Higgins did that through a content franchise. You can also do collaboration posts on Instagram, duets and stitches on TikTok, and more.

Emily Cole, the Duke athlete from earlier in the chapter, went viral and saw huge gains in her followers after another college athlete responded to a funny reel she put out looking for a date to a formal. She said she only had 8,000 followers when NIL began, but after a series of reels back and forth with Ohio State lacrosse athlete Mitchell Pehlke – who ultimately drove seven hours to go to her formal – her account started to get some attention.

Cole has been creating Instagram reels and TikTok videos consistently since her viral formal content, and less than three years later, she has nearly 200,000 followers on Instagram and over 321,000 on TikTok. This has allowed her to work with major brands like Therabody, H&R Block, Dick's Sporting Goods, and Champs.

While you may only have a four-figure following now, you can grow your numbers – and your NIL deals – if you start being consistent with your content creation like Cole was. And while going viral can feel like it's all about luck, you can't go viral without putting new content out there.

Bottom line: Getting free products and services or inking those cash deals is going to require some work, and if you're not up to that, it's okay. Go back to Chapter 2 and take a look at all the other ways you can monetize your content.

But if you're ready to get consistent, at the end of this chapter my business partner Leah Clapper (a former UF gymnast) has content ideas she first shared on our NIL Island platform for athletes for those days when you have no idea what to post.

Utilizing Content Franchises

Content franchises are a great way to force yourself to be consistent and also build your own unique brand. Take Higgins, for example, the Division III volleyball athlete who partnered with Lululemon for her Instagram live interview series. When Higgins landed her first

NIL deal in high school with Q-Collar, she had just 1,300 followers. By the time she landed Lululemon less than two years later, she had increased her following to more than 11,000 followers.

How did Higgins grow her following? She credits much of it to her "W4LKING and T4LKING" interview series, a weekly content franchise she was encouraged to create during her time in Meta's NIL Empower 2.0 program. You can bet if the people who work for Instagram's parent company are advising creating this kind of regular content series, it's probably a good idea.

"Laney's a great example of how hustle, hard work and being proactive are key elements to success in the NIL era," said Wathen. "As a DIII athlete, she's had to be intentional about building her audience on social media and finding NIL opportunities. One strategy to help athletes grow their followings is creating a 'content franchise,' a repeatable/thematic/episodic series that you do on a consistent basis and keeps your audience wanting to come back (interview series, weekly day in the life, etc.)."

In the first season of her series, Higgins featured 20 female student athletes who had a combined social media following of over 1.2 million. That means Higgins was getting in front of the audiences of all those other female athletes, no doubt earning her new followers. She also turned this live content into recap reels on the platform, generating over 140,000 additional views.

"Laney's *Walking and Talking* franchise is a great example of this that has helped her share valuable information, tap into new audiences (by going live with other athletes), and create a franchise that brands can integrate into," said Wathen. "This series, combined with her professionalism and proactiveness reaching out to brands, helped her land a sponsorship with Lululemon where she now integrates the brand naturally into the content."

So here's the good news for you: Anyone can do what Higgins did. It doesn't have to be an interview series; it can be any consistent,

99

Social Media Marketing

thematic/episodic piece of content. Former Stanford basketball athlete Fran Belibi did hers solo as "Thinky Thought Thursday," where she shared whatever was on her mind. Many of her weekly sessions were relatable struggles or stories that either made people feel less alone or inspired them to take action.

Whether or not you decide to create weekly episodic content like Higgins and Belibi, the one thing you can't ignore if you want to be able to land social media deals is consistency. Nothing is more important than putting out consistent content.

Building a Community for Long-Term Success

Green says the key to growing your brand on social media is to convert your followers into a community:

> *Going viral and having a ton of views is great, but the athletes who end up running their brand full-time post-college (whether as a content creator, entrepreneur, or both) are the ones who really engage with their audience. The athletes who brought their audience along with them throughout their entire collegiate journey are the ones who will carry that audience with them after they graduate because their audience fell in love with them for who they are, not just the sport they played.*

She says the easiest ways to build communities is through Instagram Broadcast Channels and Instagram Stories. These platforms allow you to bring your audience behind the scenes and give opportunities for additional engagement through tools like polls and quizzes.

Most users are familiar with Instagram stories, which allow users to share photos or videos that disappear after 24 hours (unless they're saved to a highlight). They are vertical in format, filling your phone screen, and allow users to add stickers, emojis, filters, and more. You can also engage with your followers by adding a poll, quiz, or even ask a question that followers can reply to directly from your story.

Fewer athletes are using broadcast channels on Instagram. These are a public, one-to-many messaging tool, almost like a group chat. However, the creator can turn off comments from others in the channel, add polls, go live, and more. It allows you to connect with your most engaged fans.

Another option on Instagram is paid subscriptions. In exchange for a monthly fee, fans can see exclusive content (lives, stories, posts, or reels) and receive a purple badge by their username when they comment on your posts or send you DMs. You can also connect with up to 30 in an exclusive chat.

Choosing Your Social Channels

As of this writing, Instagram and TikTok are the most popular platforms for athletes to be active and monetize their content. Green also encourages athletes to take advantage of LinkedIn and X: "X is where hyperlocal sports fans go to search for the latest news on NIL and sports play-by-plays. This is the platform where athletes can connect with superfans. Many of my athletes join 'Twitter Spaces' with local sports podcasts and actually end up landing NIL deals because of it."

Tying in with the advice you'll find in the following chapter on finding the right person to pitch at a brand, Green encourages athletes to be active on LinkedIn:

> The majority of people hiring athletes for NIL deals, such as heads of influencer marketing, are on LinkedIn. Very few athletes are publishing on LinkedIn, so those who take advantage of it face less competition compared to other platforms. I have my athletes post about ways that brands can work with them on LinkedIn, as well as their experience working with other brands.

101

Social Media Marketing

Post Ideas for Athletes

Do you struggle with what to post? Clapper has a great list of ideas on NILIsland.com for different types of content you can rotate:

Transformational Reels and Posts

- String together clips from each year of doing your sport.
- Show when you first started your sport versus now.
- Do a drill then show the skill.
- Share last year's highlights versus this year.
- Show a fail video versus a success video.
- Document practice versus competition.

Motivational Reels and Posts

- Share a voiceover about the biggest goals you set and the journey you took to achieve them.
- Share the biggest challenge of your sports career and how you overcame it.
- Share a past failure and how you turned it into fuel for later success.
- Sync clips of your athlete life to a motivational speech audio.
- Tell people how you deal with fears, doubt, or uncertainty.
- Use a quote from a coach or teammate as inspiration.
- Share a motivational lesson you've learned.

Funny Reels and Posts

- Show an embarrassing moment from a game or competition.
- Caption silly photos or videos from your sports career.

- Show the not-so-great sports photos you've gotten.
- Tell a funny story from your athletic career.
- Share silly POV memes related to athletics.

Behind-the-Scenes Reels and Posts

- Voiceover or text-to-speech of what you're thinking during a game/competition.
- Share something you don't think your audience knows about you/your sport.
- Show the process of getting ready for a game/competition behind the scenes.
- Answer commonly asked questions in a video.
- Show the drills you do on a regular basis.
- Share your warm-up or conditioning routine.
- Share your sports superstitions.
- Share media day behind the scenes.
- Share travel day behind the scenes.

Lifestyle Reels and Posts

- Get ready with me for a practice/game/competition (hair/makeup/talking).
- Sync various clips from your day to a trending audio.
- Vlog throughout a practice session.
- Vlog a game/competition day.
- Show the process of getting ready for practice.
- Share what you eat in a day.
- Show your morning routine.

103

Social Media Marketing

- Show your evening routine.
- Offer a day-in-the-life peek.

Friends and Teammates Reels and Posts

- Have your teammates imitate an athlete or coach from your team.
- Have each of your teammates try a crazy or viral athletic move.
- Ask each of your teammates silly interview questions.
- Capture random moments – teammates in the wild.
- Film a fun contest (race, strength competition, etc.).
- Remix/duet one of a teammate's videos.

Getting Verified on Instagram

One of the top questions I hear from athletes is about how to get verified on Instagram, otherwise known as the "little blue check-mark." This badge helps confirm that the person is who they say they are. Many believe it's a credibility booster that can help them land more NIL deals.

As of this writing, there are two ways to get verified: (1) purchase a paid subscription to Meta Verified, or (2) apply to be verified based on being deemed a notable person. The paid subscription is only available to those 18 or older.

Most athletes are interested in pursuing the application process to become verified without having to pay for a subscription. The application will ask for an identification document (such as your driver's license or passport) and information on why you're notable. Currently, the application has a field to describe your audience (who they are, what they're interested in, and why they follow you) and three links to articles, social media accounts, or other links that show your account is "in the public interest." It also notes: "Paid or promotional content won't be considered."

Those links are the most important part of your application, says Wathen:

> *These should be articles, stories and press where the athlete is the primary subject matter (i.e., a feature story, not just a link to your athletic roster, social handle, etc.). Factors such as follower size, athletic ability, videos, and links to other social media platforms do not help an athlete's chances of being verified; it is largely based on external sources written about the athlete (notability) as well as basic requirements such as ensuring the account is authentic (account must represent a real person), complete (must be public, have a bio, and at least one post) and unique (must be the unique presence of the entity it represents).*

If you have been written about already, here's Wathen's advice for how to choose the three links you submit:

> *Unique features from national or local newspapers, their university website and national publications such as ESPN, Yahoo Sports,* Sports Illustrated, *etc. The more notable the source/outlet, the better. These features should be unique/ independent (i.e., don't include the same feature from five different sources). Including a range of features will give the athlete the best chance of success.*

If you don't get approved, however, Wathen says not to get discouraged. You can reapply every 30 days, so if you receive more media coverage later, it's worth trying again.

If you're over 18, you can also opt for the Meta Verified subscription instead. Some are hesitant to pay for verification, but it

105

Social Media Marketing

comes with account support that can help you recover your account if it's hacked. If you're making money on your Instagram account, it's important to protect your business. Check with your accountant, because this may also qualify as a business expense for tax purposes.

"Verification isn't required to find NIL success," said Wathen. "By being consistent, engaging, and proactive reaching out to companies, you can still find success capturing brands' attention."

Key Takeaways

- Your social media profile is valuable real estate and makes the first impression on potential brand partners. Focus on creating a professional, consistent profile with a clear username, high-quality profile photo, and compelling bio that reflects your personal brand.
- Balance "algorithm-based content" designed for virality with "brand-building content" that supports your long-term goals and helps attract partnerships aligned with your future plans.
- Brands value athletes who foster genuine community engagement over those with large but passive audiences. Use tools like Instagram Stories, broadcast channels, and interactive features to build connections with followers.
- Each piece of content should align with one of your three "brand buckets" (see Chapter 3) to reinforce your personal brand and attract relevant opportunities.
- Keep a list of content ideas for those days when inspiration is lacking. Mix transformational, motivational, funny, behind-the-scenes, lifestyle, and team-focused content to maintain variety.
- The most successful athletes on social media share genuine content that represents their true interests and personality rather than what they think brands want to see.

Chapter 5

Finding Deals, Pitching Yourself, Pricing, and Negotiations

The vast majority of high school and college athletes engaging in NIL are doing so without an agent or other representative to pitch them. Some are relying on third parties like marketplace platforms and collectives (more on both of these in Chapter 6), but the ones I've seen be most successful are doing some outreach of their own.

In this chapter, I'm going to share with you how to find deals and my pitch framework for reaching out to brands, including the things I think can set you apart in a pitch. Then I'm going to show you real pitches from athletes who landed deals and have graciously agreed to share those pitches as examples for you. And finally, we'll cover pricing yourself and negotiating the final deal.

Where to Find Deals

Maybe you've already got an established social channel or two, and you're ready to start finding deals. If you have more than 1,000 followers on Instagram/TikTok or YouTube, you should be able to start finding brand partners. It might not be Nike or Mercedes, but local businesses and smaller brands are definite options.

What if you're under 1,000 followers right now? There are definitely athletes who land deals before they hit 1,000, but you might want to spend time focusing on finding your audience first with the tips discussed in the last two chapters on personal branding. Figure out what you want your personal brand to represent, and then start creating consistent content.

Let's say you're already over 1,000. What then?

One of the first things every athlete ready to get started with NIL asks me is how to get an agent. But that's not the first question you should be asking. Instead, the first question should be: Do I need an agent for NIL?

The short answer: It depends. Agents are generally most helpful for well-known "star" athletes and athletes with large social media followings. If you feel overwhelmed by inbound NIL offerings (i.e., your DMs are blowing up), it may be a good time to search for an agent. (We'll dig into more about agents in Chapter 8.)

Marketplaces

If that doesn't sound like you, however, there are a couple of options for finding deals. First, there are companies widely referred to as "NIL marketplaces," which are platforms where brands post deals that athletes can apply for, and athletes can maintain profiles so that brands can find athletes with the attributes they need for a campaign. Dozens of companies have been founded to help student-athletes find and secure NIL deals, and many companies that already worked with professional athletes or influencers have started new divisions or platforms to cater to college (and, in some instances, high school) athletes.

Most of these platforms focus on social media marketing, but others may connect youth athletes to college athletes for training videos or lessons, allow athletes to connect with fans for shout-out videos or to create subscription channels, provide digital storefronts for merchandise, and more.

Chapter 2 discussed several of these platforms where athletes have found success through a variety of NIL opportunities. However, we've also seen marketplaces come and go in this space over the years. For that reason, it makes sense to list yourself on as many as you can.

108

The Athlete's NIL Playbook

These types of marketplaces have existed in the influencer social media marketing space since long before NIL. Although they are not specific to athletes, you may find you have even better luck on non-athlete platforms because you stand out from the crowd.

Marketplaces allow you to post a profile that brands can search when they're seeking partners. On many platforms, brands also post campaigns you can apply for. The process to sign up is usually pretty straightforward, and it only takes a few minutes to connect your social channels, upload a photo, and enter a short bio. (You can follow the same advice given for social media profiles in Chapter 4.)

Keshawn Lynch, a football athlete at Old Dominion and then Norfolk State, has found success on several marketplaces. With Postgame, Lynch had deals with CVS, HEYDUDE, Gillette, promoting a Migos song, and the *Champions* movie trailer. He also worked with C4 Energy and Hot Topic through 98 Strong and Liquid IV through MOGL.

Because it's so easy, I recommend signing up for multiple marketplaces. Even if you aren't actively applying for campaigns that might be listed on the platform, having your profile there allows brands to find you when they're searching by keyword for athletes with specific hobbies or attributes.

Some platforms are specifically for athletes and others serve the broader influencer space. Your athletic department may have even signed on with a third-party company like Opendorse or INFLCR to create its own marketplace. Although companies may come and go, and several have merged or rebranded, these are some platforms where athletes have told me they've found deals and had good experiences:

Athlete-focused platforms

- PlayBooked
- PostGame

- 98 Strong
- Icon Source
- Opendorse

Influencer platforms

- Influential (which has an NIL division, too)
- Intellifluence
- IZEA
- BrandBacker
- Upfluence
- Aspire

You can find an updated list of active marketplaces at: https://www.athletesnilplaybook.com/marketplaces.

Shani Idlette, a Division II tennis athlete at Clark Atlanta University with just over 2,000 followers on Instagram, landed one of her most impactful deals via marketplace PlayBooked with H&R Block. "I had just jumped from undergrad to graduate school and started grad school in January. A lot of things ended up happening with my scholarships, and it was a whole mess," Idlette said on a panel with me at the NCAA Convention in January 2024. "When they gave me this deal, it gave me the opportunity to not have to take out a loan. I think in Division II, we use this money for things that we really need."[1]

Josh Africa, a golfer at Division III Penn State Harrisburg, says he did six deals with PlayBooked in his first year on the platform. Three companies he connected with there – FlightPath, Cash App, and ZipRecruiter – helped him afford a trip to play at St. Andrews in Scotland for the International Series, part of the Asian Tour. "Through NIL," he explained, "I was able to pay for travel, hotel, and other expenses I couldn't have done out of my own pocket."

The biggest thing to look out for with marketplaces is that you aren't committing to an exclusive relationship. Reputable platforms in this space do not require that. Not only is it acceptable but it's actually advisable to create a profile on multiple platforms to increase the chances that a brand or fan can find you.

Some marketplaces offer another benefit you can take advantage of: contract creation. If a brand contacts you via DM and tells you they don't have a contract, or asks you to provide one, you can bring the deal onto a platform like Opendorse and use their form contract. This also allows you to take advantage of being paid through the platform to reduce issues collecting payment on your deals. Typically, the brand will pay a fee to complete the deal on the platform, so it doesn't come out of your earnings.

Collectives

Another avenue for finding deals for those of you in college is through an NIL collective. These third-party organizations are usually tied to helping athletes at a specific school, although their organizational structure and mission can vary. (We'll talk more in Chapter 6 about NIL collectives.) For example, some focus on a single sport while others work with athletes in every sport. Some focus on working with charitable organizations and pay athletes to promote the charities or work on-site at events. Then there are ones that help match local businesses with athletes for campaigns.

If there is a collective supporting your university, it makes sense to find out how they work with athletes like you. If your athletic department has an NIL director, or someone in a similar role who has spoken to you or your team about NIL, I would ask them what they know about working with the collective.

If you don't have someone like that at your school, reach out to the collective yourself. As they say, it never hurts to ask!

Here's an example of something you could email them:

My name is Savvy Abbott, and I'm a freshman softball athlete here at State University. I'm interested in learning more about how you work with State University athletes.

I'm a marketing major with a passion for affordable fashion. I love sharing my hauls from local boutiques and online shops with my budget-conscious followers on a weekly basis. On the field, I'm currently the starting second baseman for State University, and I was named to the 2021 Los Angeles Times *All-Star team last year before entering college. You can find me on social media below.*

Instagram: @SavvyAbbott (1,244 followers) TikTok: @SavvyAbbott (1,312 followers)

Please let me know if I can set up a time to speak with someone about how I might work with you all in the future.

Sincerely,

Savvy Abbott

Before we move on to the second major way you can find deals, let me give you one last piece of advice. Make sure you're checking your DMs and email inbox(es) regularly. Dozens of brands and local businesses have complained to me that they've reached out to athletes and never received a reply. Make sure you aren't missing out on opportunities that are already at your fingertips.

Proactive Outreach

The second way you can find deals is to start proactively reaching out to brands. You already have dozens of brands you use or frequent on the daily, from clothing to restaurants, protein bars to energy drinks, and much more. Sit down and make a list of the brands you already love with which you'd like to work, and then use the pitch examples in this chapter and the next to reach out to them.

If you're a little nervous, take some advice from bestselling author Nora Roberts: "If you don't go after what you want, you'll never have it. If you don't ask, the answer is always no."

Rayquan Smith, a football athlete at Norfolk State and then Virginia State (both Historically Black Colleges and Universities, or HBCUs), sent out 100 emails to brands to get started with NIL in 2021. Ultimately, he received three responses, including one from what would become his first brand partner, Smart Cups.

That deal quickly led to more deals, and by the fall of 2023, Smith had nearly 90 NIL deals, earning him the nickname the "King of NIL." He's worked with major national brands that include Coach, CVS, Pedialyte, and Crocs.

"Don't let anybody tell you you can't get NIL deals at a smaller school," Smith said in an interview with *Business Insider*. "You could be on the bench and still get deals. It's all about how you market yourself outside of sports."[2]

Jack Betts, who was a Division III football athlete when NIL began, had a similar experience. He says it all started with a "Why not me?" mentality and the willingness to reach out to brands. He says he was sending 10–15 emails a day at one point, reaching out to brands that were already working with athletes:

> *The way that I would reach out to some of these brands is, "Hey, I noticed that you don't really have any Division III athletes in your portfolio. Why don't you let me be that pilot? Why don't you allow a possible partnership between us to be a way that you can really understand the type of value that Division III athletes and smaller market, nonrevenue athletes can bring to your brands?"*

Betts thinks what really sets him apart is having higher engagement levels than some of the Division I athletes with larger followings. His outreach has paid off, too: through the first three years of NIL, he did 40 deals, including working with major national brands like Omaha Steaks, Allbirds, Invesco QQQ, and Sprayground.

Hopefully by now you're convinced that you need to shoot your shot. Before we talk about whom to reach out to at a brand, and how to reach out, we need to lay the foundation:

- Follow the brand on all your active social channels.

- Engage with their posts by liking and commenting, and on Instagram you can reply to a story here and there.

- Tag the brand in any posts that include them. For example, if you eat at the same taco restaurant every Tuesday, take a photo of your lunch and tag the restaurant next time you're there.

Brands love when you're already a fan! Working with someone who already knows the brand and wears/uses/eats it is ideal. But how will they know that if you're not engaging with them?

Personally, my favorite strategy is tagging the brand in an Instagram story. That's because it works well with our next step: reaching out to the brand.

The How and Who

The easiest way to reach out to a brand is through their social media. I most often see this sort of interaction work on Instagram, but you could try it on any platform. What I love about Instagram, however, is that when you DM them, they'll see in the DMs where you've tagged them previously in stories!

Reaching out by DM sometimes gets you to the right person immediately, because the same person managing their social channels is

114

The Athlete's NIL Playbook

responsible for working with content creators. Other times they'll give you a contact for the correct person or even a link to an application.

You can also reach out by email. Sometimes brands have a page on their website about working with influencers or ambassadors, so I'd do a search on their website and look in places like the footer of the page.

If you don't find anything there, head over to LinkedIn. Go to the brand page, and then search through the people who work for the brand. Common job titles that indicate people who work with content creators include:

- Influencer Marketing Coordinator, Manager, Director, or Specialist
- Social Media Coordinator, Manager, Director, or Strategist
- Digital Media Manager or Supervisor
- Content Manager

From there, finding their email address can take a little sleuthing. My first try is to search the person's name and the company URL. So if I was looking for Mary Armstrong at Old Navy, I might search "Mary Armstrong @oldnavy.com." Often this brings up a good result.

If that doesn't work, my next trick is to look for other people who work at the company and have a public email address to give me the format. These are often on a press page or advertising page, because companies generally give out contact info for media looking to cover the company or someone wanting to buy advertising.

Generally speaking, company emails follow standard formats, so you can also just try the different variations until you get an email that doesn't bounce back:

firstname.lastname@companyurl.com

firstinitial.lastname@companyurl.com

115

Finding Deals, Pitching Yourself, Pricing, and Negotiations

firstname_lastname@companyurl.com

firstname@companyurl.com

lastname.firstname@companyurl.com

The Pitch

So what do you say when you reach out? Here are a few key points I would hit in every pitch:

- Who you are
- Why you want to work with them
- How you can work together
- How you're going to bring value
- Examples of previous posts and/or other partnerships

Here's a real pitch Clapper sent to land a paid deal with a local salad restaurant that follows this framework:

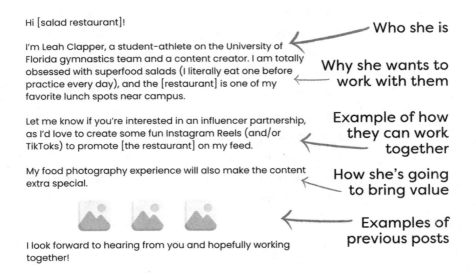

One of the biggest mistakes I see in pitches is focusing on what *they* can do for you. Instead, you need to focus on what *you*, and your audience, can do for them. This is the most important part of your pitch!

Here are some examples of how you can point out what you can do for them:

- As you saw in Clapper's pitch, it might be your photography or video skills. Are you known for a specific aesthetic or style? Great, show them that.

- If they make equipment/gear specific to your sport, it'll obviously be a point in your favor that you play that sport, but even better if you can tell them that a significant portion of your followers play that sport as well.

- Look at their recent posts and advertising campaigns. Are they geared toward a specific audience? For example, maybe it's clear they're targeting women in their teens and 20s and most of your followers fit that demographic. If so, point out in your pitch that most of your followers fit this and could benefit a product/service like theirs.

A simple email can land you a deal with even the biggest of companies. When Laney Higgins was approaching the twentieth episode of her W4LKING AND T4LKING series, she wanted a presenting partner for her second season, which would be her next 20 episodes. Because it's a content franchise built around female student-athletes getting ready for practice, games, or walking to class, she thought an apparel/shoe partner would be best:

I ranked my top 30 apparel companies and shoe companies and had Lululemon ranked number one. I began reaching out to companies in my priority order. I sent a cold email outlining my idea and pitching myself to one of the top executives from Lululemon by literally guessing different email formats for their email address.

One of the email combinations I tried must have worked, because she forwarded my email to a manager at Lululemon, who ironically was in attendance at the NIL Summit, where they had heard me speak a month or so earlier. During my speech, I talked about how my dream was to get the series sponsored. I then had a Zoom with the manager and did a really detailed PowerPoint presentation pitching my idea.

Higgins said it took several more follow-up calls and Zoom meetings with more presentations, but she finally received a contract offer, which she negotiated before finalizing. (We'll cover more on contracts and negotiations in Chapter 9.)

The time and effort Higgins put into her content series before reaching out to Lululemon, in addition to the process to land the deal, was considerable, but also worth it. "Naturally, I'm so excited that all of my time and effort paid off, especially considering they are my dream brand and that I'm able to have their help in supporting these amazing female student-athletes that come on the show," she said.

Although Higgins had just over 10,000 followers at the time of the deal, which was an impressive increase from where she started at 1,300 with her first NIL campaign, she obviously didn't get the deal based on following alone. Thousands of other college athletes have more followers than Higgins. What they don't have, however, is her W4LKING and T4LKING series. That's why it's important to focus on your own personal brand and what makes you unique instead of chasing follower counts.

Rayquan Smith began his NIL journey by cold-pitching 100 brands. He said only three replied, but that was enough to get the ball rolling and start doing NIL deals.

Here's the email pitch template Smith was willing to share:

Subject: Collaboration Opportunity with Rayquan Smith

Hi [Brand Name] Team, my name is Rayquan Smith, a student-athlete at Virginia State University, and I am reaching out to explore a potential collaboration with [Brand Name]. As a dedicated athlete and social media influencer, I have a growing following of engaged fans who trust my recommendations. I am impressed by [Brand Name]'s commitment to quality and innovation, and I believe that together, we can create impactful content that resonates with my audience and promotes your products effectively. I am particularly interested in [specific product or campaign], as it aligns perfectly with my personal brand and values. I would love to discuss how we can work together to achieve mutual benefits.

Please let me know if you are interested, and we can set up a time to discuss this further.

Thank you for considering this opportunity. I look forward to the possibility of collaborating with [Brand Name].

Best regards,
Rayquan Smith

Smith said he focused on creating quality content from there to attract new brands, and eventually he was able to sign with an agent who helped him land bigger deals. He's worked with national brands such as Eastbay, Body Armor, G.O.A.T. Fuel, Arby's, and Coach and secured nearly 100 NIL deals as of the summer of 2024.

Despite not being a household name or playing at a major Division I institution, Rayquan says there were five keys to his NIL success:

1. **Persistence:** "I didn't wait for opportunities to come to me. I actively reached out to brands, even if it meant sending out hundreds of emails. My persistence paid off when a few companies responded positively."

2. **Authenticity:** "I made sure to be genuine in my pitches and on social media. Brands appreciate authenticity because it resonates more with audiences. I showcased my personality and values, which helped me stand out."

3. **Niche Appeal:** "Being at a smaller school, I had a unique story and a different kind of appeal. Brands are always looking for diverse voices and perspectives, and I leveraged that to my advantage."

4. **Engagement:** "I focused on building a strong, engaged following on social media. It's not just about the number of followers but how engaged they are. Brands noticed that my followers were genuinely interested in my content."

5. **Strategic Partnerships:** "Signing with an agent helped me navigate the NIL landscape more effectively. My agent, Freddie Berry, had the connections and expertise to help me land bigger deals."

Smith's parting advice for athletes: "Don't be afraid of rejection. Every 'no' is just a step closer to a 'yes.' Keep learning, adapting, and pushing forward."

Email Pitch Template

You've seen some examples of pitches already above, but let's break a pitch down into a template anyone can use to pitch any potential partner.

Greeting

Keep it simple – for example: Hi [contact name or brand],

Paragraph One: Introduction

This is where you'd introduce yourself with your name, school, sport, and anything unique about your personal brand or audience, especially as it pertains to the brand you're pitching. For example, if you're an avid fisherman with an audience who is also interested in fishing – and you're pitching a related brand – this is the place to say it.

Paragraph Two: Why this brand

Do you already use this brand? What do you love about it? What does your audience love about it? Explain to the brand why you're a good fit to work together. Bonus points if you can prove it. Remember what I said earlier about posting about the brand before you reach out? If you had a post that included them and did particularly well, share a link and tell them about the analytics for that post.

Paragraph Three: The campaign

Share your idea for the partnership, being as specific as you can. Detail which platform it will be on and your vision for the photo, video, or other piece of content. Tell the brand how it will benefit them, not how it will benefit you. One of the top mistakes I see in pitches is the athlete focusing on the wrong party.

Closing

Close by saying you'd love to set up a time to chat more about your idea or their current marketing goals, and then thank them for their time and consideration.

Sincerely, [You]

If you don't hear from the brand within a week or two, I think it's perfectly appropriate to follow up one time. Emails end up in spam, or put aside and forgotten, so it's always helpful to pop it back to the top of their inbox. However, I wouldn't follow up immediately or more than once.

To follow up, forward the original email and say something short like this:

> *Hi [contact name or brand],*
>
> *I wanted to follow up on my proposal below. I'd love to schedule a time to chat further about this or how else we might work together to further introduce my audience to your food/product/service.*
>
> *Sincerely, [You]*

Pitching by DM

Youth athlete Reese Lechner (mentioned in more detail in Chapter 1) reaches out to brands from her own account, but she makes it clear that brands should communicate with her mother, if they're interested.

"Since I monitor her social media, we work together to reach out to brands/companies," said Hannah Lechner. "I'm surprised by how many companies respond. Most have replied that they are inspired by Reese and her story but 'for legal reasons,' they ask her to reply when Reese is 18 years old. We include 'please email my mom' so marketing teams feel comfortable responding to an adult versus a child. Unfortunately, even most companies don't realize youth NIL is legal."

Hannah and her daughter agreed to share the simple template they use to reach out to brands via DM on Instagram:

> *Hi @(Company) – Would you consider an NIL deal with me as a 12-year-old (trust me, it's legal)? Your market could expand with kids and athletes like me! I have a couple NILs/ambassador deals now and would like to add your company/products. If you are interested, please email my mom at [email address]. This is one article about*

122

The Athlete's NIL Playbook

me being the youngest female NIL. I hope to hear from you either way: https://www.postbulletin.com/sports/10-year-old-stewartville-girl-signs-her-first-nil-deal.

How Most Deals Work

Once you've connected with a brand over DM or email, they'll likely set up a phone or video call with you. Occasionally they may go back and forth with you over email, but it usually takes a call to get into the details.

Once you start discussing what the partnership will look like, there are a few things you'll want to cover. First, what exactly are you going to do for the brand? What type of post(s) and what platform(s)? How many posts? What guidance will they give you in terms of aesthetics or messaging? Will there be personal appearances or any other kind of NIL usage in addition to the social posts?

You'll also want to discuss the timeline. How soon do they want this content up, and do you have time to create quality content in that timeframe? Will it stay up indefinitely or for a defined period of time?

And, of course, what's the compensation? This can take the form of free food, products, services, or straight cash.

Negotiating the Deal

This is the stage where negotiation comes into play. What if you don't like the terms they propose?

When it comes to the content itself, it's important to understand the brand's expectations. Ask questions like:

- Why do you see me as a good fit for this campaign?
- What are your goals for this campaign?
- What metrics would make it a success for you?

123

Finding Deals, Pitching Yourself, Pricing, and Negotiations

It's important to know the answers to those questions so you know whether you can reasonably deliver on their expectations. The best brand deals are the ones that renew and become long-term partners.

One of the biggest mistakes I see athletes make is agreeing to create or post brand-created content that isn't a fit for their audience. From the aesthetics of the photo to the messaging of the caption or video, brand-created content can be problematic because it doesn't have your personality or authenticity, which is what your audience will resonate with the most.

You know better than anyone else what works with your audience. It is perfectly appropriate to respond in a respectful manner and let them know what you think might work better with your audience.

For example, let's say you're negotiating with a build-a-bowl restaurant and they suggest using a stock photo they have of their bestselling bowl, but you know that your posts with the highest engagement are on reels where you're actively demonstrating something.

You could respond and say, "That is a great photo, but my highest engagement comes from reels where I'm taking my audience behind the scenes. I would suggest that I visit the restaurant and order the bowl you'd like to feature so I can video the process of putting the bowl together and edit the video into something my audience will love."

Pricing

The biggest point of negotiation, however, is usually the compensation. Now, if it's a deal you got on a marketplace, there may be no room for negotiation. Some brands hire dozens or even hundreds of athletes off a marketplace to promote something like a movie opening, and everyone is getting the same flat fee. It's a take-it-or-leave-it situation. Group licensing is similar (discussed further in Chapter 7).

However, if you're negotiating with a brand you reached out to directly, or who reached out to you by email or DM, there's usually some back and forth on compensation. So how do you know how much to charge?

There are many online calculators out there that will calculate your rate based on which platform the content is going on and how many followers you have. Unfortunately, they usually don't factor in your engagement rate, and they definitely don't factor in other things like your audience that's perfectly in their niche, any exclusive rights they're requesting, or other unique details of the deal. These calculators can give you a starting point, though, so think of them as a baseline.

You might assume that the bigger your audience, the more desirable you are to brands. However, that isn't true. As the previous chapter discussed, some brands focus on micro-influencers or even nano-influencers because of their high engagement rates.

One agent I know tells people to double whatever number comes to their head or out of an online calculator. Go big or go home!

The Elements of Pricing

I personally like to start by asking them their budget. More than once I've done this with speaking engagements and had them come back with a number far larger than I would have said. You can ask by saying something like, "What is your budget for this campaign?"

Keep in mind these factors that should warrant more money from the brand:

- Exclusivity (a specific period of time when you cannot work with their competitors)
- Category expertise (meaning it's a topic you post on often or have specific experience with as an athlete)

Finding Deals, Pitching Yourself, Pricing, and Negotiations

- A link or mention in your bio (that's valuable real estate!)
- The brand's usage of your content on their own channels, website, or other marketing materials
- Costs of any materials you have to purchase (flowers, balloons, food, etc.) or any travel required

When you're deciding on whether the price that the brand has offered is acceptable, factor in the time you'll spend communicating with the brand, any additional research you need to do on them and their products/services, how long it will take you to create the content, and how long it will take to edit the content, post it, and promote it.

Taking one photo can sound like an easy way to make a buck, but I know an influencer who got asked to do 11 edits by the brand. The $100 they initially offered her didn't seem like that great a deal after the countless hours she spent going back and forth with the brand and reshooting before they finally approved photo number 12.

A Pricing Formula

Brittany Hennessy has led influencer teams at major companies including Hearst Magazines and managed over $100M in creator partnerships. She is the author of *Influencer: Building Your Personal Brand in the Age of Social Media* and now helps creators build sustainable businesses through her online community, the Influence Suite.

Numbers are often thrown around in the NIL space about how athletes have higher engagement rates than other influencers and therefore command higher rates. Hennessy says that's often true, but what she says matters more are these considerations:

- Conversion ability in specific categories
- Brand safety/reputation management

- Long-term partnership potential
- Cross-platform presence

Instead, the premiums athletes charge over other influencers might include things like:

- Category expertise (e.g., sports nutrition, equipment)
- Performance credentials
- Local market dominance
- Multi-year potential

Hennessy starts with a base price and then adjusts for exclusivity and expertise. Following is a breakdown of what that looks like by platform.

Social Media Content Creator Pricing Guide

Instagram

Content Type	Base Price
Feed post	$100 per 10,000 followers
Reel	$9 CPM (cost per thousand views expected)
Stories	$7 CPM (cost per thousand views expected)

Adjustments

Factor	Multiplier
Exclusivity	
No anticipated opportunity loss	0.3× base price

(continued)

(continued)

Factor	Multiplier
Few opportunities declined (2-5/month)	3× base price
Many opportunities declined (6+/month)	7× base price
Expertise	
Rarely create content in this niche	25% of base rate
Sometimes create content in this niche	50% of base rate
Often create content in this niche	75% of base rate
Mostly create content in this niche	100% of base rate

Additional Premiums for Athletes

- In-season content creation
- Game-day content (subject to athletic department restrictions)
- Team/conference restrictions
- Future pro potential multiplier

TikTok

Scenario	Base Price
High follower count, low views	4% of your follower count
Low follower count, high views	$15 CPM (cost per thousand views expected)

Adjust for exclusivity and expertise using the same multipliers as Instagram.

YouTube

Content Type	Base Price
Integrated video	$125/hour + $30 CPM (cost per thousand views expected)
Dedicated video	$225/hour + $30 CPM (cost per thousand views expected)

Adjustments

Factor	Multiplier
Exclusivity	
No anticipated opportunity loss	0.3× base price
Few opportunities declined (2-5/month)	3× base price
Many opportunities declined (6+/month)	7× base price
Expertise	
Rarely create content in this niche	25% of base rate
Sometimes create content in this niche	50% of base rate
Often create content in this niche	75% of base rate
Mostly create content in this niche	100% of base rate

If you are creating content for the brand to post on their social channel(s) and don't have to post it on yours – also called user-generated content – you'd charge an hourly rate instead. Hennessy suggests starting at $75.00/hour and increasing as you gain experience.

Some brands might ask you to sell the rights to a photo, and some influencers do choose to sell those for a flat fee. However, Hennessy advises against ever selling the full rights to a photo if you're depicted in the image, because your image might be even more valuable two years from now. Instead, you can license it to them for a year at a time with an annual fee.

Check out Hennessy's complete NIL pricing calculator at http://theinfluencesuite.com/nil.

Although I wanted to provide a pricing framework for you here, the truth is that pricing is always evolving, and there's no one-size-fits-all formula. Former college athlete Chloe Mitchell, who founded PlayBooked and still works regularly with brands herself, says one of the best things you can do is talk to other athletes:

> *The industry is constantly evolving, and my advice today is quite different from what it would have been even last year. Unfortunately, there's no simple formula for athletes to calculate their worth. My main recommendation is to connect with other creators and practice rate transparency. Knowing what others at your level are charging is essential for understanding your market value and ensuring you're not underselling yourself, especially for female athletes, who often undervalue their worth.*

Although I've touched on negotiation in this chapter, please read Chapter 9 on contract terms for a more in-depth lesson on exactly what you need on paper to protect yourself in terms of both the campaign and your future rights to your content and your name, image, and likeness. You might be surprised at the sneaky terms that end up in some contracts that can follow you for years to come!

Key Takeaways

- Athletes can find NIL opportunities through marketplace platforms (where brands post deals that athletes can apply for) or through proactive outreach to brands they already use and love.
- Effective outreach pitches should include who you are, why you want to work with the brand, how you can work together, how you'll bring value, and examples of previous partnerships or relevant content.
- The most successful pitches focus on what you can do for the brand, not what the brand can do for you. Highlight your audience demographics, engagement rates, and how your content aligns with their marketing objectives.
- Regularly monitor your email and social media DMs. Many brands report reaching out to athletes and never receiving replies, so don't miss opportunities already at your fingertips.
- Negotiate to maintain creative control of your content. Avoid simply posting brand-created content that doesn't reflect your authentic voice, because this typically underperforms with your audience.
- When determining your rates, factor in exclusivity requirements, category expertise, link placement in bio, usage rights, and the time investment required to create quality content.
- You can charge premium rates for in-season content, game-day content (subject to restrictions), content requiring specialized expertise, or exclusive partnerships that prevent you from working with competitors.
- Start by asking brands about their budget rather than stating your price first. This prevents you from undervaluing yourself and gives you important context for the negotiation.

Finding Deals, Pitching Yourself, Pricing, and Negotiations

Chapter 6

Working with Third Parties: Collectives, Marketing Agencies, and More

When athletes gained rights to monetize their NIL, a new economy began to spring up around college sports. Numerous third parties entered the space to help athletes make the most of their new opportunities.

In this chapter, we'll take a look more specifically at collectives, marketing agencies, and others playing integral roles in the NIL market. Beyond explaining who these parties are and how you work with them, we'll also cover issues you may encounter and how to avoid situations with negative outcomes.

Collectives

What Is an NIL Collective?

One of the most impactful developments in NIL was the formation of NIL collectives. The term "collective" as used here refers to organizations formed to source or provide NIL-related benefits to student-athletes.

The models vary, but the basic premise of most is that a group of alums band together to form a company whose goal is to provide NIL opportunities to student-athletes of a specific institution. We've also seen a few focus on a larger subsection of athletes, such as HBCU athletes or female athletes, but the vast majority support athletes of a single institution.

Where the models really differ is in how these collectives find or provide NIL opportunities. Some of the first collectives were based on low monthly memberships that any fan could join. In fact, the term "collective" comes from the very first of these organizations to form in September 2021, the Gator Collective (which supported University of Florida athletes until it dissolved in 2023 to make way for another group called Florida Victorious). In exchange for a monthly fee, fans received benefits, such as the ability to attend Zoom Q&A sessions with athletes, be entered to win autographed merchandise, attend networking events with athletes, and more.

It wasn't long before collectives realized they wanted to raise more money than a $9.99 monthly membership could support. Some collectives introduced higher monthly tiers with greater perks, while others rolled out annual or one-time tiers that ranged from hundreds to thousands of dollars.

There was one downside to collectives in the beginning, however. They couldn't offer the same charitable tax deduction an athletic department could offer to a donor because they were for-profit businesses. So new collectives were formed and applied for 501(c)(3) determinations from the IRS, and before long there were approximately a few dozen.

All these different types of collectives had the same ultimate goal: Find opportunities for college athletes so they could be paid for their NIL. Athletes were paid for online Q&As, appearances at local restaurants, signing autographs, attending fan fest events, and other activities. Collectives solicited businesses and matched them with athletes who could produce social media content featuring the brand, appear at their business to meet fans, and more.

The nonprofit collectives had to do things a little differently in order to carry out the charitable missions they were required to have in order to qualify for their tax exemptions and offer donors tax deductions. Most solicited donations from fans and boosters and then used that money to pay athletes to help promote local charities. For example, an athlete might post about a fundraising campaign for a local food bank or they might put in service hours at Habitat for Humanity. The fan or booster would get a tax deduction and the satisfaction of doing something for both the athlete and the charity. (Note: Nonprofit collectives will likely cease to exist following the *House* settlement, which is an agreement between the NCAA and current and former college athletes that aims to compensate athletes for lost NIL and other revenue opportunities and includes language that effectively prohibits the current business model of these collectives.)

Then came the big money boosters – sometimes individuals and sometimes booster-owned businesses – offering seven-figure matches for memberships or donations made to collectives.

In November 2022, Hoosiers for Good and Hoosiers Connect (two collectives supporting Indiana University athletes) announced that an anonymous donor would match every dollar donated to Hoosiers for Good or paid for sponsorships/memberships for Hoosier Connect before the end of the year. In April 2023, Florida Victorious launched a $2 million match campaign for the month of May 2023. In April 2024, two local businessmen made a $1 million matching donation to the 502 Circle (which supports University of Louisville) in support of the men's basketball team. There are many other examples; this type of matching campaign has become more the rule than the exception.

Although this section attempts to generalize information about collectives for educational purposes, the truth is that NIL collectives vary greatly from one organization to the next. Some have full-time staff members, a board of directors, and eight-figure fundraising goals. They're signing contracts with individual athletes for millions of dollars. It's not uncommon anymore for a starting QB with a Power 5 football team to receive multiple millions from a collective before even committing to an institution. (Although technically NCAA rules prohibit "inducements" like this, the NCAA was enjoined from enforcing these rules in early 2024 by a federal judge in Tennessee.)

Although the million-dollar deals are generally limited to football and men's basketball, the first softball athlete received a seven-figure deal in July 2024 when NiJaree Canady signed a one-year deal for $1.05 million with the Matador Club, a collective supporting Texas Tech.[1]

Others are run by volunteers and focus more on matching up the local pizza joint with an athlete who can post about them on social media in exchange for free meals.

Working with an NIL Collective

Chapter 5 offered a sample email you could send to proactively reach out to a collective that supports your institution. However, some of you may also have collectives reach out to you during the recruiting process or after committing to your institution.

Athlete relationships with collectives not only vary from one collective to the next, but also from one athlete to the next. For example, a collective might sign five-, six-, or seven-figure deals with some athletes that last for an entire season, or year, and require a list of deliverables, such as two personal appearances during the season and three Instagram posts per month. That same collective might also work on a one-off basis with athletes in other sports, such as paying a three-figure flat fee to a gymnast to show up at a fan fest event.

No matter what a collective offers you, there should be a contract that outlines your responsibilities, and any deliverables, as well as the length of the contract and other important terms we'll discuss in Chapter 9 that apply to all NIL contracts.

One warning story is that of Jaden Rashada, who filed a suit against the University of Florida's head football coach, Billy Napier, director of player engagement and NIL Marcus Castro-Walker and

136

The Athlete's NIL Playbook

booster Hugh Hathcock over a failed NIL deal that resulted in his signing with Arizona State instead. Rashada's lawsuit shows that he initially committed to the University of Miami for a reported $9.5 million NIL deal. He then changed his mind and signed an NIL deal worth $13.85 million over four years with the Gator Collective.

Rashada was to receive $500,000 of it as a signing bonus on December 5 in exchange for social media posts and autographing items. From there, Rashada would receive $250,000 a month as a freshman, $291,666.66 a month as a sophomore, $375,000 a month as a junior, and $195,833.33 monthly payments as a senior. In exchange, Rashada would have to meet the following obligations:

- Reside in Gainesville, Florida
- Post at least one branded Twitter post and one branded Instagram post monthly
- Appear in at least eight fan engagement events per year up to two hours each
- Autograph up to 15 pieces of merchandise annually

Later, it was revealed that the Gator Collective terminated the contract one day after the signing bonus was due (but not paid). The contract does allow for termination by the collective, but only for certain reasons. The lawsuit says the termination letter did not state any of these reasons.

After the termination, the lawsuit says that the defendants in the case continued to make him promises, including a promise from Coach Napier himself that he would receive $1 million if he signed with UF on National Signing Day. Rashada was told the original deal would still happen, but instead through the Gator Guard collective.

Florida booster Hathcock wired $150,000 to Rashada so he could repay money he'd previously been paid by Miami booster John Ruiz, who founded NIL marketing platform LifeWallet. However, no new contract for the $13.85 million was delivered to Rashada before National Signing Day. Regardless, Rashada did sign after the $1 million promise from Napier and texts from Castro-Walker saying Napier would "get it done" and saying Napier might walk away from Rashada if he didn't sign the letter of intent.

Rashada never enrolled at UF in January 2023 as expected, and on January 17 he was released from his letter of intent. In his lawsuit, Rashada claims the defendants "attempted to strong-arm" him into an NIL contract for far less than the original $13.85 million after he'd signed the letter of intent and given up multi-million-dollar deals from other schools.

As of this writing, the case is still pending in federal court.

Rashada's story is far from the only one about collective or coach promises made and not kept. UNLV quarterback Matthew Sluka announced in September 2024 he was redshirting for the season because of unfulfilled promises, with plans to transfer. "I committed to UNLV based on certain representations that were made to me, which were not upheld after I enrolled," Sluka said on social media. "Despite discussions, it became clear that these commitments would not be fulfilled in the future. I wish my teammates the best of luck this season and hope for the continued success of the program."[2]

His agent, Marcus Cromartie, told ESPN that Sluka was verbally promised "a minimum of $100,000 from a UNLV assistant coach for transferring there." However, once he enrolled, Cromartie said there was no effort by the collective to formalize a contract. Months later, he says the school and collective offered $3,000 per month for four months. To that point, all he'd received was a $3,000 relocation stipend.

In December 2024, six former Florida State men's basketball players filed a lawsuit against their former coach, Leonard Hamilton. The players allege Hamilton promised them – verbally and in writing – $250,000 each that was never paid.[3]

138

The Athlete's NIL Playbook

Other situations involve estimates instead of outright promises. USC safety Marquis Gallegos arrived on campus in the spring of 2024, having been told by the House of Victory collective his baseline earning potential was approximately $75,000, according to his father. However, in April 2024, his father told *Los Angeles Daily News* that he didn't have a contract with the collective yet.[4] By July 2024, House of Victory posted Gallegos on their Facebook page as one of the athletes affiliated with the collective.[5]

Other parents were quoted in the *Los Angeles Daily News* article anonymously, all expressing their frustration with the recruitment process at USC, wherein they felt like valuations didn't match later earnings. "It's like a handshake," one USC parent said. "And when you handshake, and it's Lincoln Riley on the other side and USC, you think to yourself, 'Well, they got money, right? We're not going to get (expletive). They're good for it.'"

The director of House of Victory, Spencer Harris, chalked it up to miscommunication in the days before the federal court injunction allowed the collective to offer contracts to recruits before enrollment. "If we can't be in the conversations and educate properly, and even be the ones having the conversations, it's going to result in issues and misinterpretation of value and expectations," Harris told *Los Angeles Daily News*. "So I do think, with some of these rules evolving, it'll benefit some of these problems that have occurred."

Another parent told *Los Angeles Daily News* their son chose USC in spite of a lower valuation than other schools because of an apartment and car offered in addition to the cash. However, once the player was on campus, House of Victory offered the player half of what had been discussed during their pre-enrollment visit. The contract specified both passive and active income, which included a monthly payment for House of Victory to use his NIL and the remainder to be paid based on deliverables like social media posts and personal appearances.

The parent said the apartment soon became a burden when the player was forced to pay his rent from the money provided by House of Victory (instead of being offered in addition to it). The parent also said payments became inconsistent and the athlete racked up late fees on his rent. Eventually, they received the full value of the contract.

Harris declined to comment on any of the specific complaints in the *Los Angeles Daily News* article, saying each contract was unique and that payments aren't salaries and shouldn't be expected to be the same amount every month.

This information isn't being included here to point fingers at anyone. Instead, I want to emphasize the importance of getting all terms memorialized in a written contract signed by all parties involved. As you can see from the Rashada case, even that doesn't solve all problems or misunderstandings, but it does provide a greater degree of protection and evidence you can use should a lawsuit be necessary.

A contract should make clear how much the athlete is getting paid, when, how, and in exchange for what deliverables. There are, of course, other terms that are important, but those should be crystal clear.

Information you're relying on from verbal discussions, texts, and other communication should all be incorporated into the final contract. This is not a nice-to-have; it's a must-have.

Attorneys who regularly review NIL contracts can be found at https://www.athletesnilplaybook.com/attorneys.

One other important note: The terms of the *House* settlement require that payments from third parties who are "associated entities or individuals" (including collectives) engage with athletes for fair market value, although as of this writing, no one knows how FMV will be determined. This assessment is subject to a neutral arbitration system.

What to Know Before Signing a Collective Contract

Although collectives serve an important role in the NIL ecosystem, there's no governing body or national standards regulating their actions outside of the legal system. They're also out of the reach of the NCAA, meaning only you or your institution and its coaches and administrators can be punished for the actions of a collective. And although they have to abide by state and national laws, there's still a lot of wiggle room for bad actors or even well-intentioned collective founders and employees where things can go wrong.

What follows in this section is not intended to be legal advice but is provided for educational purposes only. Athletes are urged to have an attorney licensed in their state review any contracts before signing both for issues discussed here and for others that may occur on a case-by-case basis.

Darren Heitner, an experienced attorney in the NIL space who helped form the very first collective, has a few issues he warns parents and athletes to watch for – or negotiate – in collective contracts:

- The collective shouldn't have the unilateral right to terminate the contract and cut off all future payments.

- Any rights you give to the collective should be as narrow as possible, which should include being limited in scope, not perpetual, non-sublicensable, and not irrevocable.

- You don't want the collective to be able to unilaterally restrict you from engaging with third parties.

- You probably don't want the collective becoming the agent for the athlete, particularly on an exclusive basis.

- You also probably don't want the collective taking over all group licensing negotiations on your behalf.

Heitner also shared that one collective contract he reviewed had a clause that required the athlete to notify the collective if the athlete received any communication that tried to persuade the athlete to transfer or sign with another collective.[6]

We're going to get into more about what common contract terms mean – and what they look like in contracts – in Chapter 9. However, here we're going to hit on some that are most common in collective contracts, as opposed to other types of NIL deals.

> *Example 1: Athlete grants to [Collective] the right and license to use Athlete's name, image, and likeness in perpetuity, in any and every form.*

This clause is an example of a few issues. It's vague, broad, and in perpetuity. Basically, the athlete here would be giving the collective the right to use their name, image, or likeness in any manner forever. If you're being paid a flat fee, it's unlikely enough to cover all of that. Even if it was a sum appropriate for such a transaction, you would be allowing an organization that may change its mission – and be staffed by completely different individuals – to profit off of you forever.

What if you become a star professional athlete and your value in 5 or 10 years looks totally different than it did when you agreed to this deal? What if you end up in a completely different line of work and don't want to be associated with the school or collective anymore? What if you don't want your face on an advertisement or product you don't agree with?

This isn't the kind of clause any athlete should agree to sign.

> *Example 2: Company desires to have exclusive rights to the Athlete's name, image, likeness, and other related qualities in conjunction with their commercial, marketing, advertising, or other business activities or operations activities,*

which shall include but shall not be limited to: exclusive rights to market Athlete's personal appearances, commercial appearances, brand ambassador rights, memorabilia, trading cards, paid radio/TV interviews and podcasts, non-fungible tokens, bobble-heads, hand-signed and electronically-signed autographs, and apparel (T-shirts, hoodies, jerseys, hats, towels, etc.).

Although this clause uses far more words, it has similar issues. The only thing it really swaps out is perpetuity for exclusivity. So they aren't asking for the right to use your NIL forever, but they are asking to be the only one with those rights. That means you can't sign an NIL deal with anyone else.

Many times when I've seen contract clauses like this included in a collective contract, it's because they've advanced money to the athlete and want the ability to recoup it. Another clause in the contract will say that all revenue the collective generates from the athlete's NIL will belong to the collective until the collective has recouped its advance. This could mean that the athlete receives no funds until the advance is repaid to the collective, or some contracts set a percentage of each deal that repays the advance, with the remainder going to the athlete.

Example 3: During this Agreement, if Athlete creates or develops a logo or design (with or without Collective's assistance), Athlete grants Collective the exclusive right to sell and market any merchandise, apparel, or media featuring such logo or design on Collective's website in perpetuity. Compensation to Athlete from these sales will be determined by a separate written agreement.

Maybe you caught "perpetuity" already. Yes, this is another one of those granting the collective rights forever.

A parent sent me a contract from a collective with similar language, which her son had unfortunately already signed. After signing, the athlete and his best friend designed a logo for the athlete and planned to sell the merchandise on the athlete's website. However, the collective learned of the logo and explained that under the terms of the contract, only they could sell merchandise with the logo and attempted to enter into negotiations with the athlete for the compensation to be paid to the athlete from the sales.

Not only does this limit the athlete's own entrepreneurial opportunities, but it limits their ability to work with other third parties, such as Campus Ink mentioned elsewhere in this book. Without getting too far down the legal rabbit hole, there are also a lot of questions as to what would happen if the athlete and collective can't agree to the terms of the compensation in a separate agreement. This might lead to an "out" for the athlete, but it also might lead to costly legal fees as it's negotiated or as an attorney attempts to get the athlete out of the original contract term.

And again, the collective can sell this merchandise forever. So if the athlete goes on to be a big NFL star in a few years, the collective can still sell and profit off merchandise with his logo over on their site.

Example 4: During the Term, Athlete agrees to make up to four (4) promotional appearances annually. These appearances will take place at a mutually agreed upon location in [county where university is located].

NCAA rules restrict collectives from offering deals that are considered "pay-for-play," but collectives also want to protect themselves against athletes transferring and the collective still having to pay out a contract that is still within its term. So, many collectives now require the athlete to reside in the county of the university or to be able to make personal appearances in that county (which would likely be difficult if they lived elsewhere). It's also the reason we see many collective contracts limited to a season so the collective isn't exposing itself to long-term commitments with athletes who may transfer.

Another issue in some collective contracts is the percentage the collective is keeping of each deal. Cody Wilcoxson, an attorney in the NIL space, says, "I have seen some collective contracts that have a split of NIL proceeds 50/50 up to the recovery by the collective of the initial upfront payment to the athlete and then a split like 80/20 of all NIL proceeds after that. Whether intentional or not, the contract is ambiguous as to whether that is NIL opportunities the collective has procured – acting in a marketing capacity – or if that's all NIL opportunities the athlete has."

In fact, some collectives have worded their contracts to take a portion of all NIL deals an athlete engages in, even those it doesn't procure or negotiate. I had the opportunity to speak to one of these collectives, and they explained all they were doing to promote the athlete's overall brand, and therefore believed any NIL deals that went directly to the athlete were still due at least in part to their marketing and brand building.

This is not the norm, and I wouldn't advise an athlete to sign a collective contract that gives the collective a percentage of all NIL deals. Instead, the contract should limit the collective to a reasonable percentage (20% or less) of deals it brings to the table.

The most important advice is this: Seek legal counsel before signing a contract with a collective. Many attorneys offer free or affordable consultations for athletes, and a growing number of universities now offer free legal advice through law clinics at their associated law schools or through other community programs. Beware of any legal advice coming directly from athletic administrators, or attorneys associated with their department or the collective, however, because they might have a conflict of interest due to their association with the collective. You want a legal review that focuses on the best terms for you.

Working with Third Parties: Collectives, Marketing Agencies, and More

You can find a list of attorneys who regularly work with college athletes at https://www.athletesnilplaybook.com/attorneys.

Marketing Agencies

We'll discuss being represented individually by an agent in Chapter 8, but there's a growing model of collectives and athletic departments creating or contracting with agencies to help find NIL deals for athletes. It's expected this trend will grow as revenue sharing is implemented.

One highly publicized example is at Clemson University, which decided to create an in-house agency with Everett Sports Marketing. ESM is well established in representing NFL athletes and has also represented female athletes such as the Cavinder twins for NIL opportunities. The in-house agency will work to connect athletes with businesses as "brand ambassadors."

ESM previously worked with University of South Carolina through an entity called Park Avenue before the NCAA halted its operation in 2022. During the three months of that partnership, it procured over 100 partnerships for South Carolina's athletes.

Two Circles, a sports marketing agency, announced in 2024 it would begin creating marketing agencies for schools to help athletes activate marketing campaigns and provide the staff in those markets.[7]

The proposed *House* settlement also gives athletic departments the ability to act as an athlete's marketing agent for third-party NIL contracts. This can be accomplished through a relationship with a company like ESM or Two Circles, or athletic departments could start forming their own internal agencies.

Even academic departments have been putting together programs to help athletes. At Oklahoma State University, professor and veteran marketer Dr. Maribeth Kuzmeski started the Brand Squad in 2021 as a student organization where full-time students in the Spears

School of Business could get valuable experience while helping athletes grow and monetize their personal brands.

Students have to apply and be accepted to the Brand Squad, then undergo a training course, before they're able to start working directly with athletes. Oklahoma State athletes fill out an interest form and are then matched with the business and marketing students. Several students may work with each athlete, helping them grow their following and create content calendars with engaging content, in addition to helping them reach out to brands and find opportunities.

The Brand Squad has helped athletes land deals ranging from $250 to $10,000. It also helps create merchandise, including items like shirzees (T-shirt jerseys). Athletes are able to make nearly 50% of the proceeds, which is a great deal more than generally offered through group licensing. For example, in 2023, the Brand Squad had sold $80,000 in football shirzees before football season even began, with athletes receiving $11.65 per shirt sold. Today, the Brand Squad sells shirzees for every sport.

Additionally, a media team captures photos and videos athletes can use for social media or brand activations. For the nonathlete students, these opportunities provide skills training and resume/portfolio material. One hundred percent of students who've been active members of the Brand Squad have been able to land internships and jobs in sports marketing.

Other schools have spoken to Kuzmeski about adding their own Brand Squad program, and as institutional involvement is increasingly allowed, others are considering related models for students in adjacent fields like PR.

Third Parties Offering Advances

It would be impossible to cover every type of third party getting involved in NIL. However, it's safe to say that not every deal offered to an athlete is advantageous to the athlete. One type of story emerging now that the first athletes to profit from their NIL in college are now professional athletes is the matter of future earnings.

Gervon Dexter was a football athlete at the University of Florida in 2022 when he signed an NIL deal with Big League Advance (BLA). Reportedly, the deal paid him $436,485 during his collegiate years. However, the agreement required him to pay the company 15% of his pre-tax NFL earnings for 25 years should he make it to the NFL.[8]

That's a big chunk of change, so it's not surprising Dexter was tempted enough by the payday to say yes. After all, he got to keep the advance even if he didn't make it into the NFL.

Dexter did make it to the NFL, though, and his first contract was worth $6.72 million over four years. Fifteen percent of that to BLA would equate to $1.008 million, more than twice the amount he received in college. BLA can also add on a late fee of 10% plus interest if Dexter doesn't make his payments on time.

In the lawsuit, Dexter is attempting to get out of the contract because it didn't contain warning language required by Florida's Athlete Agent Statute. He also claims it violates Florida's NIL statute because it creates a relationship that extends beyond the athlete's college career.

The case is still pending in court as of this writing. However, it serves as a cautionary tale for current athletes.

BLA isn't the only company using this sort of business model to tempt college athletes into taking immediate cash at the expense of their long-term earnings. News of another company called Nilly began circulating in late 2024.

Nilly's platform offers college athletes advances on their future earnings and is run by former ESPN NBA analyst and former athlete Kendrick Perkins. As of October 2024, ESPN reported the company had deals with 20 high school and college football and men's basketball athletes.

148

The Athlete's NIL Playbook

Perkins and his co-founder, Chris Ricciardi, told ESPN the company offers athletes payments ranging from $25,000 to hundreds of thousands. In exchange, Nilly has the exclusive rights to the athlete's NIL for up to seven years. The deals vary, but Nilly receives 10–50% of the athlete's NIL earnings during that period.

The company defended its business model by saying it wanted to relieve the athletes of financial stress by providing immediate cash. Although the company is gambling on how much NIL money the athlete will eventually make, it has also set itself up for tremendous profit if the athlete does succeed. For example, one contract reviewed by ESPN gave $50,000 to a high school senior in exchange for 25% of the athlete's NIL earnings for seven years or until Nilly earns $125,000, whichever happens first. This would give Nilly a 150% return on its investment.[9]

It's better to be proactive than reactive. Many of the potential issues athletes may face when signing contracts are covered later in Chapter 9, including issues like exclusivity and payment terms. Before signing any contract with a third party, however, it's advisable that it's reviewed by an attorney.

You can find a list of attorneys who regularly work with college athletes at https://www.athletesnilplaybook.com/attorneys.

Key Takeaways

- Many NIL problems stem from verbal promises that aren't formalized in contracts. Always insist on a written contract that clearly outlines payment amounts, payment schedules, and specific deliverables.
- Avoid signing contracts that grant rights to your NIL "in perpetuity" or "forever," because these limit your future earning potential and exert control over your personal brand.

(continued)

(continued)

- Be cautious of contracts requiring exclusive rights to your NIL, because these prevent you from entering other potentially lucrative deals with different parties.
- Research collectives before signing, including speaking with other athletes who have worked with them about their reliability in fulfilling contractual obligations.
- Ensure contracts clearly specify what percentage of deals the collective or agency will receive and whether this applies only to deals they facilitate or to all your NIL opportunities.
- Companies offering large upfront payments in exchange for percentages of future earnings can seriously impact your long-term financial well-being.
- Know under what circumstances either party can terminate the agreement and what financial obligations remain if termination occurs.

Chapter 7

Licensing and Intellectual Property

Would you like to make money off jerseys with your name on them? Or maybe trading cards? If you're a football athlete, do you want to be featured in EA Sports College Football video games?

Those are all examples of what we call licensing your intellectual property (IP) or publicity rights. Your name, image, and likeness are rights you own that companies or your university will pay you a licensing fee to use. So while terms like "licensing" and "intellectual property" might not sound exciting, they are important to understand if you want to see fans wearing your jersey or playing as you in a video game.

Other types of IP might be books that you copyright or logos that you trademark. So let's first discuss what intellectual property is so you know how you can protect your rights and monetize them.

IP refers to creations of the mind that are protected by law. You might hear people refer to your NIL as your intellectual property, because the right of publicity is an intellectual property right, which can also include your nickname, voice, signature, and photographs.

Two other key types of IP you may encounter as an athlete are copyrights and trademarks. Copyright protects original creative works like books, music, art, and software from being copied or used without permission, lasting for the creator's lifetime plus 70 years. We'll dig into this more later in the chapter, but the person who creates the photo, painting, book, song, and so on owns the copyright, not the person depicted in it (although that person has their own rights).

151

Trademarks give you exclusive rights to use distinctive names, logos, symbols, colors, and designs that identify products or services, like the Nike swoosh or your university's logo.

There is a third type of IP called a patent, which gives an inventor exclusive rights to their inventions, such as devices, substances, methods, and processes. This isn't one likely to apply to many athletes, so we won't cover it here.

For athletes, understanding copyright, trademark, and publicity rights is crucial since your personal brand (name, image, and likeness) and any content you create (social media posts, videos, logos, and more) are intellectual property that can be licensed for profit.

Protecting Your IP Without Violating Someone Else's

It's important to understand when you do and don't have the right to use IP belonging to others. For example, you can't produce your own T-shirt that combines your name or image with the university's logo without the university's permission because you don't have rights to their IP. This is called co-branding, which we'll cover more in the next section.

Some common situations that require permission would be wearing your jersey, or a shirt with the school name or logo, in social media content as part of an NIL deal. Some schools also prohibit you from earning by signing an autograph on any piece of merchandise with the school name or logo.

Even using just your university's colors in conjunction with your own merchandise can present an issue. Some schools have trademarks for their colors (University of Texas for its burnt orange Pantone 159 and University of North Carolina for its Pantone 542), meaning they have the exclusive right to use them.

There was also a lawsuit back in 2004 where Louisiana State University, the Ohio State University, the University of Oklahoma, and the University of Southern California sued an apparel manufacturer that had used its colors on shirts with other elements that suggested an affiliation with the university, such as geographic location, game scores, references to events like bowl games, or slogans.

Ultimately, the universities won that case, even though none of the shirts had the university's name or logo. That means you could have an issue if you use school colors in combination with any phrase or image that suggests the university.

Most universities and athletic departments now have processes set up where athletes can request permission to use the university's IP in photos, merchandise, or other NIL ventures. Every school's policy differs, however, with some allowing more uses than others. Many also charge a fee for the use of their IP.

If you're a high school or youth athlete, your state high school athletic association may limit your ability to do NIL deals that include any reference to your school or its IP. Many of the state high school association rules that have been passed expressly prohibit NIL deals that include school IP. It's best to check in with someone at your school before proceeding.

For all athletes, it's also important to note that when you work with a third party, such as a company hiring you for social media content, you'll need permission to use the university's IP, such as if the company wants you to wear your jersey, other team-issued apparel, or even team colors in the photograph.

Some companies engaging in NIL are already university or athletic department sponsors and have rights to use the IP in certain contexts. However, you should always check with the person that handles your university's IP before agreeing to have anything that references the institution you attend in your content for NIL deals.

153

Licensing and Intellectual Property

Many institutions also require you to get their permission to use athletic facilities in your content (which are generally full of university IP on signage, walls, etc.). For example, if a company wants you to film your video in the football stadium, you should ask your athletic department if that's allowed and if there's any paperwork you need to submit, or permissions from any other departments you need, in order to do so.

Another common situation athletes find themselves in is wanting to use photos of themselves taken by others. Even though the image features you, the photograph itself is the IP of the photographer. That means you need their permission to use the photo, even just to post on social media.

Khloe Kardashian, Jennifer Lopez, Jessica Simpson, Gigi Hadid, and 50 Cent are all celebrities who've been sued by Getty Images for using photos without their permission.

The photos provided to you by your athletic department from athletic events, media days, and more are generally ones you can post to your own social media, but they do require permission to use in NIL deals since you don't own the copyright to the photograph and it likely contains university IP.

Group Licensing and Co-Branding

The good news is that universities and third-party licensing companies have been quickly evolving during the NIL era to create more opportunities for athletes to create merchandise and products that include both their NIL and the university's IP through co-branding or group licensing. Jerseys, shirzees (T-shirt jerseys), T-shirts, trading cards, and video games are some of the most common merchandise available to athletes today.

Before we dive into what these opportunities look like, what exactly are co-branding and group licensing? Group licensing allows for multiple athletes to all be part of the same NIL deal, whether that's for jerseys, trading cards, video games, or any other kind of product or deal. Each athlete in the deal is offered the same terms (including the same royalty rate or other payment), but it often creates opportunities for athletes who might not be offered a deal on their own. If sales can be tracked to a specific athlete, such as with jerseys/shirzees, the athlete is paid the royalty based on their individual sales.

In addition to group licensing, you may hear the term "co-branding." These opportunities are similar in that an athlete's NIL is used alongside the university's IP. Although these are generally still handled under group licensing deals, in some cases they could involve a separate arrangement with a single athlete.

What to Know Before Opting into Group Licensing Agreements

There are companies focused on developing group licensing opportunities for athletes, such as the Brandr Group and OneTeam Partners. You will need to opt in to allow those companies to include you in deals they put together, such as a trading card deal that includes your entire team.

These deals are usually – and should be – nonexclusive, meaning it won't limit your other NIL opportunities. While group licensing can open up opportunities for athletes outside of the most well-known or most-followed, it's not always advisable for those with higher market values because the rate isn't based on individual value.

Attorney Josh Gerben says he would advise athletes who have a big enough name to stand on their own to avoid group deals. "This is because your reputation could be tarnished if one of the athletes in the group ends up in trouble for one reason or another. Think about it like having business partners. If one partner is a bad apple, it typically ruins the entire business. The more an athlete can run on his or her own, the better."

Attorney Darren Heitner said he's also advised clients not to opt into their university's group licensing deals:

"I recall attempting to negotiate in what I believed to be a reasonable provision – 'OneTeam shall not authorize any third party to use Athlete's Identity without the prior written consent of Athlete, which consent shall not be unreasonably withheld or delayed' – for a prominent athlete only for OneTeam Partners to reject the modification and the client ultimately determined it was not worth signing the contract."

Furthermore, these middlemen often take a big chunk (30% for OneTeam Partners) from athletes before you take into consideration the athletes' fees they must pay their agents as well as monies they need to set aside for taxes.[1]

According to one of the contracts athletes have signed with one such company, the athlete is agreeing to the following:

- The right for third parties (unknown at the time of signing) to use the athlete's "name, nickname, initials, autograph/signature (including facsimilies), voice, picture, photograph, animation, image, likeness, persona, jersey number, statistics, data, copyrights, biographical information, and/or other personal indicia" for commercial use in deals that include at least three other athletes

- 70%/30% revenue split in favor of the athlete, paid twice annually

- To be part of the group licensing program until the end of the athlete's last year of collegiate eligibility or until the athlete joins a group rights program in a professional sport

This is a fairly broad grant of an athlete's NIL, and this particular agreement didn't have a clause that allowed the athlete to terminate its participation in the program prior to the end of their collegiate eligibility. However, it did allow for the athlete to give notice to the company that a use would conflict with the athlete's personal brand or existing contractual relationship with another company.

A contract from another company in this space had similar terms for the rights granted, revenue split, and term of the agreement. However, it also included some additional terms that are troublesome for athletes:

- Any "merchandise, logos, designs" created as part of a merchandise opportunity is owned by the company, not the athlete. This means that if an athlete designed a logo alongside this company for, say, a T-shirt opportunity and wanted to continue to use that after their collegiate career for other opportunities, the athlete wouldn't have the right to do so on their own.

- An irrevocable and perpetual right to use the athlete's name, image, likeness, etc. (all those rights we talked about above) in the company's promotional, marketing and advertising. This means the company can use these things forever, even if the athlete terminates the contract.

Many athletes choose to be part of these deals. For those with fewer individual opportunities, it can provide an easy avenue that generally requires little effort from the athlete. Even athletes with higher values choose to opt in because they want to participate alongside their teammates or to be part of something like the EA Sports video games.

As mentioned in Chapter 1, group licensing deals can also be an attractive option for international athletes, because this can allow you to license your NIL and earn compensation without any "work" on your part that would violate the terms of your student visa.

157

Licensing and Intellectual Property

Jerseys and Shirzees

Jerseys and shirzees are opportunities that are often available to athletes across a variety of sports. These programs can be led by the athletic department's primary apparel provider (adidas, Nike, Under Armour, etc.), third-party licensing companies (such as Learfield/ Collegiate Licensing Company, the Brandr Group, or OneTeam Partners), or any other company or retailer that has rights to the university's IP.

In 2023, it was reported that jerseys created through a partnership between OneTeam Partners and Fanatics paid a 4% royalty on jersey sales.[2] A year previously, it was reported that amounted to approximately $3.92 per jersey. Meanwhile, athletes who were part of the Brandr Group's jersey program were receiving $10–$12 per jersey, and the M Den – a Michigan-specific retailer working with Valiant – was offering $20 per jersey.[3]

Sources in the industry indicate M Den was able to do this because it bought blank Michigan jerseys in bulk prior to NIL beginning, which provided a higher profit margin and therefore allowed it to pay the athletes a higher royalty rate. However, it's worth noting that M Den filed for bankruptcy in 2024, owing the University of Michigan $8.8 million in royalties.

There is risk for those who produce and sell merchandise like jerseys with athlete names, particularly because of the transfer portal.

"The transfer portal places licensees and retailers at great risk for any pre-decorated merchandise, and individual customization isn't inexpensive as retailers either have to purchase premade nameplates or machines to cut vinyl names and numbers to add to blank jerseys, as an example," explained Marty Ludwig, associate vice president of trademark licensing and brand management at the University of Cincinnati.

T-Shirts and Other Apparel

Another popular type of merchandise created through group licensing is T-shirts and other apparel. Campus Ink is one company that has been helping athletes create and sell their own merchandise, through both group licensing and individual agreements.

As of January 2025, Campus Ink said it had paid out more than $2 million to athletes in royalties across more than 100 university partners and 20,000 athletes. The highest-earning athlete on the platform earned more than $100,000. The more athletes market their gear, the more they stand to earn. Campus Ink says it arms athletes with everything they need, including "Shop My Locker Room" graphics when their individual locker room becomes available and custom graphics when they have a new jersey or other product. The company also posts on their school-specific social media accounts, sending athletes who are active on the platforms a collaboration request.

In addition to the advantages of saving athletes from having to design, stock, and ship merchandise, companies like Campus Ink can also help athletes quickly capitalize on big moments in competition. New merchandise commemorating viral or extraordinary moments can be on the site and selling in less than 24 hours if they're already signed up with the company.

For example, when Purdue wrestler Matt Ramos defeated a three-time NCAA champion in the semifinals of the 2023 NCAA Wrestling Championships, Campus Ink dropped "Shock the World" merchandise for him the next day. When North Dakota State's Hunter Poncius, a reserve offensive lineman, blocked an extra point to lead his team further in the 2023 FCS playoffs, Campus Ink had his merchandise up the next day too so he could capitalize on the sudden attention on him.

However, it's not always smooth sailing. BreakingT attempted to help Vanderbilt quarterback Diego Pavia leverage his moment in the spotlight following his team's upset over then-number-one-ranked Alabama by producing shirts with the phrase "Vandy We Turnt," which he said after the game.

When BreakingT posted photos and a link to purchase the shirt, Pavia tweeted, "This is not me. WE HAVENT WORKED OUT A DEAL! DO NOT ORDER."

BreakingT responded shortly after saying, "Well, this is awkward. These shirts were approved and are licensed by Vanderbilt and yourself (via OneTeam Partners), and you're receiving a royalty on all sales. Please DM us if you'd like anything further. Thanks."

Unfortunately, Pavia had forgotten – or was unaware – that he'd signed a group licensing agreement that allowed for this sort of merchandise to be created and sold. He later took down the tweet.[4]

Even if an athlete's school doesn't have a group licensing arrangement that includes a company like Campus Ink, athletes can generally sign up with these companies on their own through their websites. Campus Ink's process takes less than five minutes.

Trading Cards

From print-on-demand and NFTs to traditional printed cards, many established trading card manufacturers like Topps, Panini, and Upper Deck have worked with college athletes.

Panini partnered with OneTeam Partners in 2021 shortly after rules changed to create both physical and digital trading cards for athletes across a variety of university partners, and Upper Deck had signed four individual NIL agreements by late 2022.[5]

Fanatics, which purchased the Topps brand in 2022, initially entered the collegiate trading card space the same year when it reached a deal with over 150 universities and almost 200 college athletes. A source told *Forbes* that individually signed athletes could make "well into the five figures."[6]

It hasn't just been the largest trading card companies entering the space, however. In August 2021, it was announced that then–Georgia quarterback JT Daniels signed an exclusive trading card deal with Super Glow that netted him $100 per signature. The six-month contract reportedly netted him 50% royalties on both signed and unsigned cards, with his agent estimating the deal could reach seven figures.[7]

Even nontraditional companies jumped into the trading card game. Jacksons Food Stores in Boise, Idaho, partnered with the Broncos football team to create the first full-team trading card set of the NIL era.[8] Media company TexAgs announced in 2022 it would be producing its own football trading cards.[9]

Although trading cards are often associated with male athletes, companies have signed both top individual female athletes and entire teams to deals since NIL began in 2021.

LSU gymnast Livvy Dunne, the most-followed athlete in college sports, secured a deal with Leaf in 2022, which she expanded in 2023 to include a collection of signed memorabilia. Her teammates Elena Arenas, Savannah Schoenherr, and Aleah Finnegan have also worked with Leaf. The company's roster also includes other female athletes like UConn basketball's Paige Bueckers and Jackon State female football athlete's Leilani Armenta.[10]

Although Panini engaged with college athletes shortly after NIL rules were changed in 2021, it launched a new platform called Panini College in 2024 that will allow all athletes who opt in at their partner universities to have their own trading card, with the program kicking off with football and volleyball.

Panini has also been offering deals to high school athletes, offering them multi-year deals before they even enroll in college.[11]

ONIT, a new player in the trading card space, is focused on signing whole teams, not individual athletes. Women's teams like Florida women's gymnastics, Ohio State women's hockey, and Nebraska women's volleyball have all had team-wide deals.

Although royalty rates differ based on sales channel, ONIT told *Extra Points* it pays approximately $3.50 to athletes for each of its packs, which retail for $12.99. Some athletes also get the opportunity to serve as ambassadors to promote the products, which carries with it an additional payment above the royalty rate.[12]

Video Games

The EA Sports *College Football* video game was discontinued in 2014 due to lawsuits over athlete compensation, but the changes in NIL rules allowed it to return in 2024. This group licensing opportunity was facilitated by OneTeam Partners and was offered to more than 11,000 FBS football players (all eligible scholarship football players on all 134 FBS teams). By March 2024, more than 10,000 athletes had opted into the game.[13]

News of the fee each athlete would receive – a flat $600 plus a complimentary digital code for the game – had many wondering if star athletes would agree to be in the game. However, EA Sports did broker separate marketing agreements with what was reported to be approximately 200 football players to promote the game for fees that ranged from four to five figures.

Arguably one of the most – if not the most – marketable football athletes in the country, Arch Manning, agreed to the deal after initially opting out.

Some interesting terms in the contract included:

- A term that runs through the athlete's last college football season, although athletes can opt out during a specified period each year
- The right for EA Sports to use an athlete's slogan or logo in the game without any additional compensation
- Photographs coming from the universities, meaning athletes wouldn't be able to provide or approve the image used of them
- A statement that opting in didn't obligate EA Sports to put the athlete in the final game
- Waiving the right to participate in any future lawsuits with respect to the agreement[14]

EA Sports is also expected to bring back its college basketball game, previously called *NCAA Basketball*.

Other Group Licensing Opportunities

There are many other creative group licensing deals you may have the opportunity to take part in as an athlete. One that made news with UNC's men's and women's basketball athletes was the NIL FanBox, which was facilitated by the Brandr Group.

NIL FanBox is a subscription box made available to fans that includes memorabilia, including some autographed items. Athletes are compensated for the use of their NIL in items such as posters, photographs, and more.

The first NIL FanBox with UNC in late 2021 included all eligible members of UNC's men's and women's basketball teams, who gathered together over a couple of days to autograph items for the boxes. In total, $100,000 was distributed to the athletes who participated.[15]

This is another group licensing deal where international athletes could benefit from passive income, although they wouldn't be able to be compensated for autographing any items, only for the use of their NIL on items in the box.

Group licensing can also be used to coordinate social media marketing across a group of athletes from different sports and schools. For example, the Brandr Group worked with 15 members of the FSU softball, LSU women's basketball, TCU women's soccer, Michigan women's track and field, and Georgia women's volleyball to share their experience sitting in the Liv Más Student Section via TikTok.[16]

By mid-2023, temporary hair color company Hally Shade Stix had worked with nearly 250 student-athletes across 70 schools in nearly every sport through group licensing. When the brand launched its yellow and green colors, it partnered with the Baylor women's basketball team and over 100 athletes from other sports, in addition to working with players in the SEC softball championship.

Sony Music worked with the Brandr Group and influencer platform Pearpop to sign a group of UGA student-athletes to promote Kane Brown's release of the single "Bury Me in Georgia." The athletes were from a variety of sports and created "day in the life" videos on TikTok featuring the audio.[17]

Group licensing is an area that is only expected to increase going forward as more companies see the value in working at scale and engage in new campaigns.

Trademarks

Trademarks help protect certain of your brand elements under both state and federal law. For example, athletes can register trademarks for their names, nicknames, slogans, or logos.

Attorney Gerben says athletes should file a trademark application for their nickname, logo, or slogan as soon as possible. That's because trademark rights in the U.S. are based on first use. You can file an application on an "intent to use" basis or later provide proof of when you first started using the phrase or mark. Note that international trademark laws vary and don't necessarily follow the same guidelines. If you're an international athlete, or are an American athlete who plans to use your trademark internationally, you should consult with a legal expert in your country.

Legal protection begins from the day the application is filed with the USPTO, although Gerben says it takes approximately 14 months to go through the entire registration process.

Having your trademark registered can make your licensing deals more lucrative. "The main drawback to making these filings is the cost," said Gerben. "Even when using a smaller law firm, the filings can cost $2,000–$3,000 per application (including government fees). This is sometimes a deterrent to making the filing. But as soon as financial resources allow, trademark filings are the gold standard in brand protection and should be pursued."

Once you have a trademark, Gerben advises athletes to focus on two things: on-field success and off-field likability:

"The most successful licensing deals come from athletes that have the brightest lights shining on them. Ultimately, the combination of a star athlete with a good personality is the most marketable. This is why LeBron James, Travis Kelce, Peyton Manning, and Tom Brady are in so many commercials. Not only are they great athletes, they are well-liked humans with solid reputations. You typically don't see the athletes who have personal or legal trouble in commercials because no brand wants to be associated with the off-the-field problems."

Jason Kelce is a great example for athletes to follow, suggests Gerben. "He was a little-known player in Philadelphia until his on-field play and off-field personality (particularly his outfit and speech during the Super Bowl parade) endeared him to the city. He could sell almost anything to any Philadelphian. Then his brother, and subsequently his brother's relationship with Taylor Swift, pushed him into the national spotlight."

Obviously, we can't all be Jason Kelce. However, you can take advantage of the spotlight you do have as a high school or college athlete and the popularity you have in your own town.

"Most athletes are local stories first," Gerben explains. "If they can become beloved in the town in which they play, they can begin to build a brand to sell products locally. Then, if they are lucky, an event occurs that pushes them into the national spotlight. Having a brand that has been successfully building locally, and then can rise to the national level given the opportunity, is the goal. This is also how almost every small business begins, grows, and ultimately scales."

The key is to focus on your branding, particularly your own branded merchandise, Gerben says. Instead of simply promoting other businesses, start building your own business that can scale and grow as you do. Then if you or your team end up in the spotlight, you're already in a position to take advantage of it.

Having a registered trademark also requires you to maintain continuous use and file renewals with the USPTO. For example, there's a filing due between the fifth and sixth years after the registration date, another between the ninth and tenth, and then every ten years after that.

Getting a trademark approved isn't always easy. Others may have already registered the same words or mark or something similar and object after you apply. For example, UConn women's basketball athlete Paige Bueckers attempted to register the phrase "Paige Buckets" but later abandoned the application after an opposition was filed by another trademark holder of other "Paige" marks.

If you're thinking about coining a phrase or nickname, first do a quick check at https://tmsearch.uspto.gov/search/search-information. This will allow you to see any active trademarks. Note that if you do see someone else has an active trademark, it may only be for certain categories. For example, it might only list "educational services," which means they don't have the trademark on clothing items with that trademark. At this point, you'd want to get advice from an attorney who practices in the intellectual property space.

One athlete I helped navigate the book publishing process had to change her book title at the last minute after I did a trademark search and found the phrase she used for her title was already trademarked by someone else. Unfortunately, you can't use someone

167

Licensing and Intellectual Property

else's trademark on your products or merchandise without their permission. Luckily, the book hadn't gone to print yet, so she was able to change it.

Athletes should also give thought to the words and marks that define their personal brand before trademarking them. Former University of Florida quarterback Anthony Richardson used the nickname "AR-15" and created merchandise with this branding before later moving way from it because of the association with gun violence.[18]

It's also important athletes maintain control of their own trademarks and don't allow them to be held by agents, collectives, or other third parties.

NBA athlete Luka Dončić even had to file a petition against his own mother to wrestle back control of his trademark and register additional trademarks. His mother owned "Luca Doncic 7," and Luka found he had trouble registering for trademarks for "Luka Doncic" and "Original Hoops of Luka Doncic" because the United States Patent and Trademark Office found those trademarks were confusingly similar to "Luka Doncic 7."

Although he had given his mother permission to file for the trademark when he was 19, he wanted to revoke that consent at 23 to regain control and file the new trademarks. He later dropped the petition and was said to have privately resolved the matter.[19]

Trademark is a complicated area of law, but there can be huge financial consequences if you misuse someone else's IP. For anything involving your university's name, logos, or images, check with someone in your athletic department, or in the office that handles university IP, for advisement. If you're ready to monetize your own nickname, slogan, or logo, consult with an attorney who practices in this area.

A list of attorneys who regularly work with college athletes is available at https://www.athletesnilplaybook.com/attorneys.

Key Takeaways

- Your name, image, and likeness are publicity rights you own, while copyrights protect creative works, and trademarks protect distinctive names, logos, and symbols you create. Consider filing for trademark protection for your nickname, logo, or slogan as early as possible. Rights in the U.S. are based on first use, and registration provides stronger protection.
- To avoid complications later in your career, ensure that trademarks are registered in your name, not held by agents, collectives, or other third parties.
- You cannot use university logos, colors, or other trademarked elements in your merchandise or promotions without permission. Always check with your athletic department before using any of these in NIL activities.
- Even when you appear in a photo, the photographer owns the copyright. You need permission to use photos taken by others, especially for NIL deals.
- Group licensing deals allow multiple athletes to participate in merchandise sales, trading cards, video games, and other products alongside university intellectual property. They can provide income opportunities with minimal effort, especially for athletes with fewer individual deals.

169

Licensing and Intellectual Property

Chapter 8

NIL Agents

Signing with an agent who can help you find and negotiate NIL deals sounds exciting to many athletes. After all, your time is limited, and you probably don't have much experience reaching out to brands to pitch yourself.

An agent can take pitching, contract negotiation, and chasing payments off your plate. A good agent will even increase your opportunities by finding you more NIL deals. Most of all, you'll have someone to get you the best deal terms and highest offers.

Unfortunately, there aren't enough agents for *every* athlete to obtain representation. The good news, however, is that not every athlete needs an agent. Contrary to popular belief, having an agent doesn't automatically mean you'll receive more NIL deals. Often you are your own best advocate.

UCLA quarterback Chase Griffin is a great example of an athlete who chose to manage his own NIL career. "I felt like nobody would be able to represent me and tell my story the way that I could." Griffin also said he was in a good position to represent himself because he had enough inbound opportunities not to need an agent out proactively looking for more.

Division III football athlete Jack Betts also found some benefits to representing himself:

> *Being an athlete who only has one televised game per year, it was a little bit more difficult to land those partnerships.*

But once I did, a lot of them began to appreciate the professionalism in which I approached every single partnership. I represented myself. I didn't have an agent, so the brand spoke directly with me. We talked through the types of content that I'd be interested in creating, the types of things that I had in mind in order to promote their brands and to promote their products. And so I think it was all about the organic aspect of it, them feeling really that it was an intimate partnership, that they didn't have to go through an agent in order to talk to me. So I think those are just some of the things that really set me apart and allowed a Division III athlete like myself to have success in this realm so heavily dominated by my division one counterparts.

With that, let's get into whether or not you need an agent.

Who Needs an Agent?

You know that age-old question about which came first: the chicken or the egg? Getting an agent is a little bit like that. Athletes feel like they can't get deals without an agent, but they can't get an agent without already being in demand for deals.

Agent Michael Raymond says any college athlete might be able to find an agent, particularly a younger one looking to build their client roster, though he does admit that landing a more experienced agent might be tougher.

So who needs an agent?

"I would say somebody in the top 100 of your sport. If it's basketball or football, potentially a first- or second-round pick. On top of that, it helps to be marketable and have a good social media presence. Someone who is getting incoming brand deals and opportunities and wants someone to handle those communications and be able to protect you and add value."

In addition to football and basketball athletes, Raymond also represents an impressive roster of female clients in gymnastics, volleyball, track and field, and more.

"Typically, we sign athletes that have major marketability. They're able to make at least six figures in NIL brand deals, and then they have another five to six figures in collective deals and other opportunities coming their way that we can help negotiate and help them leverage."

For athletes outside of first- and second-round football and basketball talent, he's looking for social media creators who are going to do at least 30–40 brand deals in a couple-year span and make six figures.

Agents aren't the only ones who can help you, however.

"It is time to seek an agent or legal counsel the moment an athlete is presented with a business opportunity," said Darren Heitner, who has represented athletes separately as an attorney and as an agent. "These individuals, commonly referred to as professional service providers, typically have the requisite experience, education, and acumen to serve as a fiduciary and act in the best interests of the athlete, providing a service that the athlete is not qualified and/or in an advantageous position to handle for themself."

You'll find more of Heitner's advice in the following chapter on contracts and legal issues. You can access a list of attorneys who regularly work with athletes on NIL contracts at https://www.athletes nilplaybook.com/attorneys.

Questions to Ask Before Signing with an Agent

For athletes who do have the opportunity to sign with an agent, you shouldn't sign with just anyone. Agents in the NIL space range from seasoned professionals with decades of experience representing professional athletes to college sophomores brokering deals for their friends.

There is no national standard or required registration process mandated by the NCAA, or other college sports organizations, and only about half the states have any kind of agent registration required by state law (and in some of those states, it's debatable if NIL representation falls under the statutes).

Having the wrong agent is worse than having no agent at all. For example, some agents take excessive percentages of deals, even if you find the deal on your own. Predatory agents may just wait around until you get offered a deal and then swoop in for their commission. This is why it's important to carefully review your contract before signing (a list of important contract terms is later in this chapter).

You should also talk to current and former clients to ensure you're signing with someone legit who isn't going to just take your money and run.

Hopefully, I've convinced you to do your research before you choose an agent. But what are you looking for? Here are several important questions to ask an agent before you sign:

- How many clients do you currently have and how do you ensure you make time for them each?
- Will you be the person working with me directly? Will there be others on your team I'll interact with?
- Do you represent any other clients similar to me? How would you handle any potential conflicts of interest?
- How many contracts have you negotiated?
- What are some examples of NIL deals you've negotiated for your clients?
- How do you proactively find me new NIL deals?
- What is your fee structure? Do you take a percentage of any NIL deals I acquire on my own? Is your percentage the same whether it's an NIL deal with a brand versus a deal with a collective?

- How would you say you've advanced your athletes off the field?

- What's your communication style? How often will I hear from you? Will I get updates or only hear from you when you have a deal to present?

- Can I send you inquiries I get from brands in my email or DMs to vet for me?

- Are you registered with the state? (For states that require agents to register, there's usually a list of current registered agents on the Secretary of State's website – try searching something like "Pennsylvania registered athlete agents" to find it. I would check to ensure the agent you're considering is properly registered to ensure you're working with a qualified professional.)

- Have you ever been disbarred, suspended, or otherwise disciplined related to your profession?

- Have you ever been investigated by the NCAA or any other professional organization?

- What services do you offer beyond contract negotiation?

- What happens to our relationship if you change agencies? Would I go with you or be assigned to a new agent at the first agency?

As you're analyzing the answers you receive, Heitner says to keep in mind the following expectations you should have for an agent:

> *A person who is going to always put the best interests of the athlete above the agent's interests. Someone who will take great interest in the mission and goals of the athlete as well as the athlete's desires and interests, coming up with a gameplan on how to best accomplish goals. An individual who has the appropriate level of experience, education,*

and track record to get the job done, never overpromising and always overdelivering. Someone who isn't in the business of telling athletes what they want to hear, but what they need to hear.

Google the agent and go through a few pages of results to make sure there's nothing online that raises red flags. Take a look at their social media. Does it look professional? Are they showcasing athlete deals?

"I think that a lot of agents don't spend any time in branding their clients at all or pitching their names out," Raymond said. "We post our deals on social media every single day. I write LinkedIn posts every single week about clients. Because why not? It's free promotion for them, and that just will lead to more deals and more money for everybody."

In addition to questioning the agent and doing some digging online, you should also find both current and former clients whom you can ask about their experience with the agent. I've found this to be incredibly helpful in my own process of hiring broadcast and literary agents, and I can usually find folks to talk to through my online research.

Here are some questions you can ask current and former clients:

- What are the agent's biggest strengths and weaknesses?
- What kinds of deals did the agent find for you?
- Did the agent explain each deal in enough detail that you felt like you understood what you were agreeing to?
- How did this agent improve your NIL opportunities?
- Is there anything you wish you had asked before signing with an agent?

- Would you sign with this agent again?

- For former clients, why are you no longer represented by this agent?

Things to Look for in Your Agency Contract Before You Sign

Ideally, you should get an attorney to look at your agency contract before you sign it to ensure it protects your interests and not just your agent's. While every contract is different, here are key pieces you absolutely must understand before signing.

Term

There should be a section in your contract that states the term of the contract. It may list beginning and ending dates or have language such as "Twelve months from the date of the Agreement," which usually corresponds to a date in the opening paragraph of the contract. It may also mention a time period from the date of signing, which would refer to a date at the end near the signature line.

Having a beginning and ending date specified is the clearest way to establish the term so there's no disagreement. For example, what if it's from the date of signing and you signed on one date and the agent signed on another?

Questions that should have clear answers in this section (or elsewhere in the contract) are:

- When does your term begin and end?

- Does the contract automatically renew? (You'd need to make note of this and the number of days, weeks, or months of notice you have to give to prevent the automatic renewal.)

- Do you get to decide on renewal or is it the agent's sole decision? (Hint: You don't want to agree to the latter.)
- Does it extend into your potential future professional career?

You should never sign a contract that doesn't have a clear term. If you receive a contract that doesn't have this, or has a vague reference, ask the agent to add something specific.

Commission

In most cases, you'll see a percentage fee the agent will take from your opportunities. Anything from 10 to 20% commission to the agent is typical (including if you're using a social media agency that typically works with nonathlete influencers). If it's more than that, I'd ask more questions about why it's higher and be disinclined to accept it.

As long-term deals with collectives become more common, and with revenue sharing on the horizon, some attorneys and agents have been vocal about 20% commissions being inappropriate for these situations.

Attorney Joshua Frieser, founder of Frieser Legal, says commission on collective and revenue sharing contracts should be more closely aligned with the standard in professional leagues like the NBA and NFL:

> I do think a 20% commission is way too high for collective and future revenue sharing deals. I think the best structure for college athletes is to have two different commission rates: 10–20% for endorsement deals and ~3–5% for collective and revenue sharing contracts. I've also seen some representation agreements structured where the agent's commission is 10–20% but only of the amount they negotiate above the 'initial offer' on a collective deal.

It's also important to note whether the agent wants all funds paid through them first, meaning they'd have the third party pay them, take out their percentage, and then remit to you, or if you'll get paid directly by the third party and then remit the agent's share to them. If you have to remit, how long do you have to do so?

Cody Wilcoxson, an attorney with Blank Rome who works in the NIL space, says he strongly advises clients to have all NIL money flow through them and then pay the agent. "The agent works for the athlete, not the other way around."

Scope of Representation

The scope of representation – which simply means all the ways the agent works with you – might be called a number of different things in the contract, but what you're looking for is what types of opportunities the agent will be taking their commission on.

Most importantly, will they take a percentage of deals, autograph signings, speaking gigs, book deals, and so on that come directly to you and don't involve them at all?

About half the contracts I've seen take their percentage on *any* paid opportunity the client is offered. Personally, I wouldn't sign that kind of deal, but you have to decide for yourself. Another alternative would be what Frieser suggested above, where commission is paid on any amount the agent negotiates above the initial offer.

Termination

The contract should include a clause that details how the contract can be terminated by either you or the agent. It's important the contract spells this out for each of you, not just the agent.

How much notice is required to terminate? Thirty days is fairly standard.

What happens to deals you're in the middle of completing or negotiating? (Spoiler alert: Usually you still pay commission on those, which can be painful if it's a long-term contract with the brand or other third party.)

While it's standard to pay commission on any deals that were signed during your term with the agent, be sure you understand the language pertinent to this. Some contracts require you to pay commission on deals that result after you part ways if the agent had conversations with the brand or "contemplated" working with the brand while you were still a client. Be very careful with this type of language so you don't end up paying commission on deals that arise after the end of your representation where the agent didn't really contribute anything.

If you're signing with an agency with multiple agents, you might also want to ask your agent what happens if they decide to go to another agency. Do they get to take you with them? Or do you stay behind at the agency and get assigned to another agent?

Unfortunately, I have personal experience with this. I had a broadcast agent I loved, but he left halfway through my network contract to go to another agency. He wasn't allowed to take any clients with him, so I was left behind and assigned to an agent I did not get along with. I could terminate the contract, but the agency retained the right to my current contract with the network and also the right to negotiate the option the network held to extend their time with me.

Let's just say it didn't go well, and now I always ask agents about this before I sign to make sure I don't get stuck in this situation again.

Disputes

Ideally, you and your agent will have a long, productive, and happy relationship together. Unfortunately, things happen.

How will disputes between you and the agent/agency be handled? Is there a mediation or arbitration clause? Where does it say disputes will be heard? Usually this is wherever the agent/agency is located, which means you'd have to travel if you aren't in the same city.

Once again, it's advisable to have an attorney review the contract before you sign it. I have named only a few of the important terms, but there are other important considerations like indemnity clauses and confidentiality clauses. I don't want to overwhelm you with legal jargon, so I simply encourage you to have an attorney review any contract you sign, including a contract with an agent.

Also, remember that having an agent doesn't guarantee you will be offered more NIL deals. Every agent's connections and successes are different, as is the time they'll devote to you and how proactive they will or won't be in seeking out deals. That's why it's important to take the time to ask the right questions so you can make the best decision for you.

What It's Like to Work with an Agent

Although Raymond says athletes should expect a lot from their agents, he also cautions athletes that NIL deals can ebb and flow. With basketball, for example, deals will pick up during the season, and particularly as you get closer to March Madness.

"In the summertime, it gets really slow. So in the summer you should be talking to your agent, or your agency, and strategizing on how you can build your brand." He suggests using downtime for things like community service events, hosting camps, attending events, and networking.

In terms of how your agent can help you during this period, they might set you up with a financial advisor for some meetings, help you set up some local events, or guide you in making more social content.

As you ask potential agents the questions posed above, be looking for answers that give you some indication of the connections they already have and how they strategize finding deals.

For example, here's what Raymond says about his own agency: "It's all about figuring out what comes next. So if March Madness is around the corner, which brands and sponsors are going to be super active during that March Madness period? We need to figure that out two to three months beforehand so we can already be pitching our athletes' names for those NIL campaigns that are going to come out."

Combine that with the fact that his agency has already done more than 1,000 deals, and you know they have a big list of contacts and a strategy they can implement.

While your agent should be bringing you brand deals, Raymond says it's also important that the athlete be putting in the work to make themselves more valuable. "There are plenty of talented athletes out there that brands can work with, who are going to post on social media, going to have a personality and not be afraid to speak in front of the camera. If you're an athlete who's not willing to put in the work just as much off the court as on the court, you're not going to have a lot of NIL deals come your way."

Above all, Raymond says you should expect communication from your agent, and they should be someone you trust.

Having the Wrong Agent Is Worse Than Having No Agent

Tikisha Gobourne, whose daughter, Derrian Gobourne, was a gymnast at Auburn who landed multiple brand deals and even got signed to the WWE NIL program, says they learned the hard way about the dangers of signing with the wrong agent:

When we first signed with an agent, we really didn't know what we were doing. We were new to the process, so we just went with the flow and placed our trust in him, thinking that he would have our best interests at heart. Unfortunately, that turned out to be the worst idea ever. He didn't deliver on any of the promises he made – whether it was negotiating better deals, providing career guidance, or securing sponsorships. To make matters worse, we later found out that he was actually stealing money from us. It was a tough lesson learned.

Even if the agent isn't stealing from you, they might be disorganized, stretched too thin, or just plain bad at the administration side of their business. Raymond says he's taken on clients after they were with other agents and had to chase down money they'd been owed for months.

"I've seen previous agencies not send proper invoices and leave a lot of money on the table. Three to four months will go by, and the money was never paid, and then I'm left trying to figure out how to get people to pay up three or four months later with a completely different agency, meaning me, because their old agents didn't send proper invoices and ask for the money."

This goes back to the question about how many clients they have and broader questions about how their agency works. Do they have support staff or is it just one person trying to do it all?

Wilcoxson also urges athletes to ask their prospective agent about their legal background or the legal support available at their agency. "There are non-lawyer agents that have been doing this a very long time and do a fantastic job, but unless you have seen how these provisions play out in the courtroom, it is difficult to give meaningful advice on whether or not a provision is appropriate in a contract for your client. If the person is not a lawyer, does the agency have an in-house lawyer they use to review the agreements? Or outside counsel? If not, how is this person assuring me they will protect my rights?"

Gobourne also cautions that just because an agent is getting you deals doesn't mean they're invested in building your long-term brand. "An agent might be more motivated by their commission than by what's best for your career. For instance, they might push for a deal that benefits them financially but might not align with your long-term goals or personal values."

Raymond says he's taken on several clients who were previously represented only to find they were locked into bad long-term deals. "I've seen agents that have signed horrible contracts that lock in exclusivity for 12 months or 24 months for a brand deal that probably lasts them about a month or two. You're looking at one video from August to September, and they're locking in exclusivity and even giving away usage rights for perpetuity purposes, giving them the usage forever."

We'll talk more about exclusivity and perpetuity in the next chapter on contracts, but it's important to note that many of the issues we talk about in that chapter could be avoided by having proper representation by an agent or utilizing an attorney well-versed in the NIL space.

Gobourne recommends many of the same questions mentioned earlier in this chapter to help separate the good agents from the bad. Derrian later signed with Raymond, and Gobourne says it's been a night-and-day difference. "From the moment we started working with him, it was clear that he genuinely cares about his athletes. He treats his clients like family and consistently goes above and beyond to ensure they are well-represented in every aspect. His integrity is unmatched, and he's shown time and again that he's fully committed to their success, both on and off the field."

184

The Athlete's NIL Playbook

Derrian isn't the only athlete to run into issues with an agent. In 2022, T.A. Cunningham, a 16-year-old high school football athlete in Georgia, transferred to California in order to earn NIL money. At the time, California allowed high school athletes to do NIL deals, but the Georgia High School Association did not.

"The Levels Team promised that the Cunningham family would have a home, transportation and meals in California," said an injunction filed for Cunningham. "A promise was even made that the Levels Team would provide a separate home in Georgia for [Cunningham's] mother."[1]

Unfortunately, four weeks into the season, the California Interscholastic Federation's Southern Section deemed him ineligible to play and told him he'd have to sit out a year. Initially, a judge denied his request for an emergency restraining order, keeping him from playing in games.

Next, the Southern Section began an undue influence investigation based on information from the court proceedings because of a bylaw that stated: "A student may not be eligible to participate at the varsity level if there is evidence the move was athletically motivated or the student enrolled in that school in whole or part for athletic reasons."

The petition in the court case made it clear he moved in order to participate in NIL. It showed that a youth coach in Orange County, who was also the co-founder of a marketing agency, helped Cunningham make his plans to move to California to take advantage of NIL opportunities and even housed Cunningham and his younger brother for a time period.

That was until the coach was arrested on multiple accounts of sexual assault of a minor. The marketing company stopped communicating with the Cunninghams, and the brothers were across the country with nowhere to live (although they were taken in by the president of the local Pop Warner league). They also hadn't experienced any of the NIL success they'd been promised.[2]

185

NIL Agents

After missing five games, the Southern Section reversed their decision and ruled Cunningham eligible.[3] They declined to make their findings public, but ultimately the athlete missed out on two games in his junior season and went through both the move and a stressful situation that could have been avoided.

Even if you end up with a great agent, it's important to stay engaged in the process and understand whom you're being pitched to, how you're being positioned, and the details of your deal.

"Relying too much on an agent can lead to an athlete becoming disconnected from the business side of their career," Gobourne says. "It's important for athletes to stay informed and involved in decisions, even when they have an agent handling the details."

Ask questions or insist on changes if something doesn't feel aligned with your brand and your goals. Remember, your agent works for you, not the other way around.

Parents, Family Members, and Friends as Agents

When asked about why he chose not to hire an agent, Griffin said he was in a unique position where he had support from his family and other people around him with the knowledge to assist.

"My father has been a great help and has run point on a lot of projects for me, especially while I'm in season. And I've just been blessed to have a family that supports me throughout this entire process and family friends who are experts in the space. So, even though I'm not represented, I'm absolutely not alone in this. And I think everyone who wants to have success in this space should have folks around them who care about them and have expertise."[4]

It's fantastic when an athlete has supportive family who can help lighten the load or even actively get involved in NIL. For example, if your mother is a lawyer, you might not need an agent to review your contracts.

However, I would be remiss if I didn't mention that having a family member manage your money or affairs can sometimes get messy.

One athlete, who agreed to share her story anonymously, told me about how her uncle acted as her agent and stole thousands of dollars from her. "My first agent was my uncle. He owns his own business, so he felt like he understood how to negotiate a contract. Along with myself, he signed a handful of other athletes. He's always been a big sports fan, and he played in college himself, so I didn't think anything about him getting into NIL when it first started."

Her uncle landed several brand deals for her with niche companies related to her sport, and he did the same for other athletes he managed. Unfortunately, she never saw any of the money. "He owes me about $21,000, but I don't think I'll ever see it."

Although there are legal remedies the athlete could pursue, her family has chosen not to do so, in part because he's family. Instead, they've distanced themselves from him, and she later signed with an NBA-certified agent she says has been fantastic.

"Now I know what an agent relationship is supposed to look like, and if I ever have to hire someone again, I know more about the questions I should ask before I sign."

NFL player and former Ohio State athlete Marvin Harrison Jr. is currently being sued by Fanatics for millions in damages for failing to fulfill his obligations to sign cards and game jerseys from a May 2023 agreement with the brand. Harrison Jr. believes there is no deal.

Although the court case has a lot of allegations we aren't going to get into here, one sticky issue is that his father, Marvin Harrison Sr., has admitted to being the one who signed the contract. "Harrison Sr. intentionally signed the Binding Terms Sheet in such a manner in order to lead Fanatics to reasonably believe that Harrison Jr. was the true signatory when in fact he was not," the lawsuit states.[5]

NIL Agents

The issue has meant that Harrison Jr.'s NFL jersey isn't available for fans to purchase, because Fanatics is the NFL's apparel provider and the NFL Players Association advised the brand, the NFL, and the Cardinals not to produce the jersey while the lawsuit is pending.

Unfortunately, there's no shortage of stories about athletes who claim family members have taken advantage of them and misappropriated funds.

Quarterback Baker Mayfield sued companies owned by his father and brother for $12 million he claimed they transferred without his knowledge.[6] Former professional tennis star Arantxa Sanchez-Vicario wrote in her memoir that her parents mismanaged an estimated $60 million over the course of her career.[7]

I'm not suggesting athletes shouldn't involve parents and family members in deals, especially if they have specialized expertise that's useful. The examples given here are similar to situations that can happen with any agent, even those who aren't family. No matter who represents an athlete, the best advice is for athletes to be involved in their own affairs at a level that would allow them to catch any concerning issues.

For a list of NIL agents, visit www.theathletesnilplaybook.com/agents.

Key Takeaways

- Not every athlete needs an agent. Consider your current demand for NIL deals, time constraints, and personal skills before deciding whether representation is necessary. Some athletes successfully manage their own NIL opportunities.
- Vet potential agents thoroughly. Ask about their experience, client roster, fee structure, communication style, and track

record. Speak with both current and former clients to understand their experiences.

- Understand what's in your agency contract. Pay close attention to the term length, commission rates, scope of representation, and termination clauses. Have an attorney review any contract before signing.
- Watch for red flags in commission structures. Standard rates range from 10% to 20% for brand deals, but should be lower (3–5%) for collective deals and revenue sharing. Be cautious of agents taking commissions on opportunities you secure yourself.
- Ideally, money should flow to you first, then you pay your agent their share, rather than the agent receiving all funds and distributing your portion to you.
- Having the wrong agent is worse than having no agent. Poor representation can result in bad contracts, missed opportunities, payment issues, and damage to your personal brand.
- Even with an agent, stay informed about your deals, understand contract terms, and monitor payment schedules to catch any potential issues.
- Expect ebbs and flows in NIL deals. Work with your agent to develop strategies for slower periods, focusing on brand building, community service, and networking rather than just deal acquisition.

Chapter 9

Contracts and Other Legal Issues

Before you skip over this chapter because it sounds boring or complicated, know that reading and following the advice in this chapter can save you from a heartbreak and frustration in the future.

Look, I get it. Contracts are super boring. Most of them are far too long, and sometimes even as a lawyer I find myself rereading a sentence over and over again trying to figure out what the heck the person who drafted it thinks it means.

A straightforward contract in writing is your best protection from being taken advantage of, misrepresented, or ripped off. Contracts outline the terms, conditions, and expectations of your collaboration. It's essential to review and understand them thoroughly before signing anything.

Contracts are more than just pieces of paper or digital documents. They serve as vital safeguards for content creators like you.

Attorney and agent Darren Heitner urges athletes to get terms in writing, preferably as part of a signed contract. "The vast majority of the disputes that I observe revolve around either poorly drafted contractual language, with ambiguity often breeding conflict, or no contractual language in writing whatsoever. If an athlete is questioning whether they should be looking for an agent or legal counsel, then it's probably the right time to begin such exploration."

If you're under 18, most state laws prohibit you from entering into a legally binding contract without a parent or guardian. State law may also require that once you reach 18, you ratify – in other words, sign – the contract within a certain time period in order for it to remain enforceable.

Benefits of a Written Contract

Understand Expectations

A written contract provides clarity by clearly outlining the terms, conditions, and expectations of your collaboration with a brand. It helps both parties understand their roles, responsibilities, and obligations. By having everything in writing, you reduce the chances of misunderstandings and disputes arising later.

Preserve Your Ownership Rights

A contract specifies the ownership and usage rights of your content. It ensures that you retain the appropriate control over your creative work and determines how it can be used by the brand. Clear usage rights protect you from unauthorized use or exploitation of your content, allowing you to maintain your artistic integrity.

One of the red flags often present in brand contracts is reserving the right to use the creator's content in future social media and marketing materials without additional compensation. Imagine you're only getting paid for one Instagram post, and then next thing you know they're using that photo on a giant poster in their store without paying you anything extra. Well, if you don't have a written contract that clearly outlines the usage rights, you may be left with no recourse.

Get Paid – and on Time

A written contract clearly defines the compensation terms, including payment rates, methods, and schedules. It ensures that you are fairly compensated for your time, effort, and talent. With a contract in place, you have a solid foundation to hold brands accountable for timely and adequate payment.

We've heard from many creators that they've submitted their invoice after creating the content only to spend months chasing payment that never comes. A written contract allows you to pursue avenues for collection much more easily than without one.

Avoid Conflict

A well-drafted contract can provide legal protection for both parties. It outlines the consequences of breaches and sets forth mechanisms for dispute resolution. Should any conflicts arise during the collaboration, having a contract can help you navigate the situation with clarity and enforceability.

Act Like a Professional

Entering into a written contract demonstrates professionalism and establishes trust between you and the brand. It shows that you take your work seriously and expect fair treatment. Brands that respect your expertise and value your contributions will readily agree to a written contract, fostering a healthier and more equitable working relationship.

Remember, a handshake or verbal agreement may seem sufficient at first, but this can leave room for misunderstandings and potential exploitation. A written contract ensures that all parties are on the same page and protects your rights as a content creator.

Understanding Contracts for Content Creators

Although the NCAA announced in early 2024 that it would develop a template contract and recommended terms, you will still be presented with contracts from brands, agents, collectives, and others who have their own contract they want to use. It's also impossible for one-size-fits-all templates or suggested terms to address everything that might come up in a deal, so you're likely still going to need to understand some of the most common issues that may arise.

Unfavorable Compensation and Payment Terms

Beware of low or unfair payment rates that undervalue your hard work. Also, keep an eye out for delayed or inconsistent payment schedules. Contracts should clearly state how and when you'll get paid, so don't settle for ambiguity.

Excessive Licensing and Usage Rights

Be cautious of contracts that give brands unlimited control over your content without proper compensation. Ensure that you have some say in how your content is used and distributed. Avoid vague clauses that grant brands unregulated access to your work.

Here are some words to look out for:

- **Perpetuity:** This means *forever*. You should only agree to this when you understand *exactly* what you're giving up forever, and you've been properly compensated for it.

- **Exclusive:** Depending on how it's worded, this usually means either only the brand has rights to the content or that you can't work with other brands in the industry (for a period of time or potentially forever).

- **Irrevocable:** If a contract, or any of its terms, are irrevocable, it means you can't later change or cancel the contract or withdraw your permission. This can leave you with limited options—or no options—should your situation, or your relationship with the other party, change in the future.

194

The Athlete's NIL Playbook

Also, look out for a long, vague list of everywhere the brand can use your content going forward. Here's an example of a problematic clause:

> *Creator grants Company a nonexclusive, royalty-free, worldwide, digital license to utilize the Deliverables **in any manner in any digital form**, including but not limited to the right to edit, alter, delete, modify, or change, in Company's sole discretion in connection with the continued promotion of the Platform, or as otherwise permitted by this Agreement. [emphasis added]*

If the price you've agreed upon is based on one Instagram post and three Instagram Stories, then you don't want to then grant them the right to use your content in other ways, such as on their social media, in ad campaigns, marketing materials, and so on. For that, you'd want to negotiate a much higher fee.

That's why it's important to make sure the contract lists exactly how, where, and when they'll be allowed to use your content. Should they wish to use it beyond those specific channels and timelines, they can come back and offer you additional compensation for those rights.

Agreeing to Be Exclusive

Keep an eye out for unfair restrictions that prevent you from working with competitor brands. Exclusivity contracts aren't automatically a red flag. It's common in these types of marketing contracts to ask you not to work with their competitors for a period of time, maybe 30 days or even six months.

Here's what one looks like:

> *It is understood that the Influencer will be working for the Advertiser on an exclusive basis for the duration of this*

Contract. It is prohibited that the Influencer post, promote, or be affiliated with any other advertiser in the following type(s) of business: beauty, personal and hair care products, makeup.

Here's how it might play out for you: Clearly Cleanser (I'm making up a company) is willing to pay you $500 for one Instagram post, but you're not allowed to work with anyone else in the beauty/ makeup industry for six months. Two weeks later, Beautiful Face offers you $1,000 for an Instagram post. You like their products better, plus they've offered you more money. Unfortunately, you can't take it if you agreed to the exclusivity clause in the first contract with Clearly Cleanser (although hopefully you followed the pricing guidelines in Chapter 5).

If you agree to an exclusivity clause, the term should be clearly defined so you know exactly when you're free to work with others in their space. In other words, it should say the specific number of days, weeks, or months you're required to be exclusive.

"I've seen even athletes with agents that have signed horrible contracts that lock in exclusivity for 12 months or 24 months for a brand deal that only lasts them a month or two. For example, they create one video from August to September, and the brand wants exclusivity long-term and usage rights in perpetuity, giving them like the usage forever," said agent Michael Raymond.

Make sure the exclusivity period is appropriate for the amount of content you're creating and the payment being offered. (Refer back to Chapter 5 for more guidance on pricing and exclusivity.)

You should also ask for a list of specific competitors instead of broad categories (like they used in the example above) so there's no confusion about whom you can and cannot work with. If they insist on using a category, try making it as niche and specific as possible, for example, "cleansers" and not the broader "beauty product" category.

You should also be getting paid more for exclusivity than if there was no exclusivity clause because it means you may have to turn down other offers that conflict during the term. (See Chapter 5 for a pricing formula.)

Right of First Refusal

A right of first refusal gives the company the ability to match offers from other companies before the athlete can sign with them. Generally, these apply after the initial term of the contract has ended.

An example is the deal then–UF track athlete Parker Valby signed with Nike in 2023, which included a right of first refusal that kicked in after her college deal ended. It gave Nike the right to match offers from other brands for six months after her final collegiate race.[1]

Normally, collegiate runners going pro announce their pro deals shortly after their collegiate career wraps. However, Valby and her father – who passed the World Athletics agent exam in June 2024 – delayed her pro signing and took the time to consider deals from other companies. Eventually, she was able to sign with New Balance instead.

These deals are becoming more common with track athletes and shoe companies, but you could find them in a variety of NIL contracts. Sometimes the brand has the right to match with a time period during which you'll negotiate in good faith (often 30 days).

Other times, it goes one step further and allows them to match any competing deal, effectively forcing you to stay with them if they match the other company's deal. Here's an example:

Athlete grants [Brand Name] a Right of First Refusal for any collaboration, sponsorship, or promotional opportunities related to brands, products, or services competing with those covered under this Agreement. The Athlete shall provide [Brand Name] written notice of any such opportunities, including material details such as the third party's name, scope of the collaboration, proposed compensation, and response timeline. [Brand Name] will have 30 days to match the terms or waive the opportunity, during which time the Influencer shall not negotiate or finalize the opportunity with the third party.

Ambiguous Deliverables and Expectations

Watch out for contracts that lack clear project briefs, deadlines, and milestones. Vagueness in expectations can lead to confusion and unnecessary revisions later on. It's important to have a mutual understanding of what is expected from both parties.

Here are two things I like to look for in my contracts with brands/sponsors:

- **"Sole discretion":** This usually gives the brand the right to approve the final deliverable. Obviously, they need to approve it. However, this term often gives them a good "out" if they want to just bail on the contract entirely. That's why I always try to get a "kill fee" – a fee I'll be paid regardless of whether or not they ultimately use my content. It tends to range anywhere from 10 to 50%, but it's better than getting nothing for your work!

- **Limit on edits:** I always negotiate for a limit on the number of edits the brand can ask for, otherwise you could end up reshooting or recreating content a dozen times or more. Most creators don't contemplate this many edits when they set the price for the deal. Limit the number of edits, and then if you and the brand still aren't on the same page, you can renegotiate or accept the kill fee (see above).

Edits

Beware giving the brand the right to edit or modify your content after creation because they could add something objectionable or not in alignment with your brand.

This is the sort of language to watch out for:

> *The right to edit, alter, delete, modify, or change*
> *At the company's sole discretion*

One influencer (who didn't want to be named) told me a disturbing story of an edit gone wrong. She participated in a photo shoot for a clothing brand. The brand shot all of the models in blank T-shirts so they could add the designs later and use the shots for multiple designs.

When the first photos landed on social media, the influencer was horrified to find herself wearing a shirt with a Confederate flag, something she didn't want associated with her brand.

Unfortunately, an attorney later told her there was nothing in her contract that protected her from this edit and no easy recourse for getting the photo removed. He was willing to pursue some legal arguments that he told her had only a small chance of succeeding, but it would have cost her significantly more than she made on the deal.

It's not unreasonable that a brand may want to reserve the right to alter a photo, perhaps for lighting, color, or even background changes or cropping. However, this should never be at the "company's sole discretion." To fully protect yourself, you'd want the right to approve any edits before photos are used publicly.

Unreasonable Termination Clauses

The biggest issue I see in creator contracts is one-sided termination clauses, meaning the brand can terminate but there is no defined process by which the creator can terminate if they decide they no longer want to work with the brand. What if the brand ends up in a big scandal you don't want to be associated with? Or maybe the person you're working with on the campaign is abusive in some way. You need a reasonable way to get out of the contract.

Termination clauses should allow either to terminate, and you should try and get a kill fee negotiated into the contract if they terminate (see above).

Use of School Logos, Colors, or Facilities

If a contract demands the use of school logos, colors, uniforms, or facilities, the brand needs to negotiate that with the school. You can put them in touch with the right person, but all rules need to be followed, and the brand should pay any fees associated with the use.

Indemnification and Liability

Pay attention to contracts that burden you with excessive legal and financial responsibilities. Indemnification refers to the act of compensating someone for any losses, damages, or liabilities they may incur. If the contract says you are indemnifying them, you need to understand exactly what you might be liable for in the future. (Honestly, this should scare you enough to get an attorney to review and negotiate it for you.)

Ensure that both parties share the responsibility for any infringement of intellectual property (which refers to creations of the mind, such as artistic works, inventions, and brand logos). You should aim for a fair allocation of risk between you and the brand.

One-Sided Contract Terms or Negotiations

Be cautious if you find yourself in a situation where the brand holds all the negotiation power. Contracts should provide a fair playing field for both parties. Don't hesitate to speak up and negotiate terms that protect your rights and value as a content creator.

If a brand makes you an offer and says, "Take it or leave it," you should probably leave it.

As a content creator, it's crucial for you to be aware of potential red flags in contracts. By recognizing these warning signs, you can protect your rights, ensure fair compensation, and maintain creative freedom. Stay vigilant, seek advice when needed, and don't hesitate to negotiate for terms that work in your favor. Your work has value, so never settle for less.

You can find more contract advice relative to specific situations in the chapters on working with collectives (Chapter 6), agents (Chapter 8), and revenue sharing (Chapter 11).

A list of attorneys who regularly work with athletes on NIL is available here: https://www.athletesnilplaybook.com/attorneys.

Quick Tips for Negotiating and Protecting Content Creators' Rights

My advice is to always consult an attorney before signing a contract, but I understand that's unlikely to happen if you're doing, say, a deal for $100 or a free massage gun. In that case, I hope you go back through this chapter and look for the issues outlined here.

Thoroughly Review and Understand the Contract
Take the time to read and comprehend every section of the contract. If something is unclear, ask for clarification before signing. Knowledge is power!

(continued)

(continued)

Seek Legal Advice if Necessary

If you encounter complex or confusing terms, consider consulting an experienced lawyer. With many NIL attorneys, your first consult is even free. They can help you navigate the legal jargon and ensure your rights are protected.

Negotiate for Fair Compensation, Rights, and Protections

Remember that contracts are negotiable. Don't be afraid to discuss terms that concern you. Aim for fair compensation, reasonable usage rights, and protections that safeguard your work.

Document All Communications and Agreements

Keep a record of all discussions, emails, and agreements related to the contract. This documentation can come in handy if any disputes arise in the future.

Key Takeaways

- A written contract provides clarity on expectations, protects your ownership rights, ensures proper payment, helps avoid conflict, and demonstrates professionalism. Verbal agreements leave room for misunderstandings and potential exploitation.
- Contracts should specifically outline what is expected from both parties, including project deadlines, number of content pieces, and quality standards to avoid confusion later.
- Terms like "perpetuity" (forever), "exclusive" (restricted from working with competitors), and "irrevocable" (can't be changed or canceled) limit your future opportunities and should be carefully considered before agreeing to them.

- Specify exactly how, where, and when a brand can use your content. Avoid broadly worded clauses that give brands unlimited rights to your content without appropriate compensation.
- If agreeing to exclusivity, ensure that the term is clearly defined with specific time limits, get the exact list of competitors, make the category as narrow as possible, and negotiate higher compensation for this restriction.
- Ensure you have approval rights on any edits to your content, or at minimum clearly define what types of edits are permitted to protect your personal brand from harmful associations.
- Both parties should have the ability to end the contract under defined circumstances. Negotiate a kill fee if the brand terminates the agreement after you've already completed work.
- Keep records of all discussions, emails, and agreements related to the contract, which can serve as evidence if disputes arise later.

Chapter 10

Growing and Maintaining Your Brand Beyond College

In earlier chapters, you might have noticed an emphasis on building a personal brand that can allow you to position yourself for success after graduation. That could mean using NIL to build skills that are relevant for your future career or even continuing to work with brands as a social influencer, booking gigs as a public speaker, and more.

Trevor Bassitt, a professional track athlete, five-time world medalist, and Olympian, returned for his final year of eligibility at Division II Ashland University in 2021 to take advantage of the opportunity to build relationships with brands (and get his master's degree) before embarking on his pro career.

"I understood that being a professional athlete is more than being an athlete. You have to be a businessman or businesswoman, and you have to figure things out that way," Bassitt said on my *Game Face* podcast in February 2022. "I've been reading books about the business aspect of sports – and I graduated with a sport management and finance degree – so, I had already started laying some groundwork for myself, for once I had turned pro, for some smaller sponsorships, smaller endorsements, things of that nature."

Bassitt spent time going around to speak to local businesses, educating them on NIL. He ended up doing four NIL deals that year, but as you'll see below, the opportunities didn't end when his collegiate career did.

"Graduating doesn't mean you have to stop being a content creator or influencer," said NIL educator Sam Green. "Many successful influencers make a living through brand deals, and you can do the same even after your athletic career ends. Start incorporating brands into your content that align with your next chapter."

Continuing to Work with Brands After Graduation

In Chapter 5, you learned about how Josh Africa was able to fund his travel to a professional golf tournament at St. Andrews in Scotland through brand deals. "This was not just my first time participating in a major golf event; it also demonstrated the increasing influence that NIL deals have on helping student-athletes pursue their career goals after graduation."

Africa says his experience while still in college helped him get a head start on working with brands as a pro golfer. "Since I finished college, my capacity to collaborate with brands has undoubtedly changed. I've effectively maintained several alliances with significant businesses by utilizing the knowledge I acquired from my NIL transactions. Not only has this proven track record assisted me in preserving these relationships, but it has also created new avenues for me to pursue in my career."

Alex Glover, a former volleyball athlete at SMU, said she found it easier to land brand deals after college. "I'm not having to plead my case as much as I did when I was an athlete. I think a lot of athletes don't know their values. So a lot of brands come at you and have such low monetization for those brand deals. I feel like now I'm more in the influencer group, and very comparable to other influencers in my group."

Bassitt said he didn't continue to work with any of the brands he partnered with in college, but that's because his value had increased.

"Once turning pro and securing a World Championship medal, my NIL value had gone up past what the companies wanted to pay so we made a mutual decision to move on."

The biggest change post-graduation for Glover isn't the number of NIL deals but the types of brands she's working with. "The brand deals I take now are more lifestyle. Obviously, when I was an athlete, it was a lot of creams and stuff to help your performance. Since I do sports content, I still see a bunch of that. So I haven't really seen a big drop-off."

Emily Cole had a similar experience. "I'm super grateful that I've still been able to work with great brands, just sharing their messaging from a new perspective as a post-grad athlete. I'm still working with running brands like Adidas and Garmin as I pursue professional track and-field. I even secured my biggest partnership deal to date with BSN Sports' SURGE program, which empowers female athletes, coaches, and parents with tools to keep more girls in sports."

As part of that partnership, the audiobook version of *The Players' Plate* (her book discussed in more detail in Chapter 2) is now available to all SURGE members, offering additional support to young athletes navigating the challenges of sports nutrition.

"I think that athletes are very uneducated on how important social media is," said Michael Raymond, an agent who represents college athletes, including Cole. Not only does Raymond think social media is key to getting NIL deals while actively playing college sports, but he says it's equally important to athletes planning to play professionally.

"Think about the NBA and the NFL. There are only about 10 to 20 athletes in each sport that are doing the commercial deals with brands like State Farm, NFL Sunday Ticket, and Gatorade. They are really talented at their sport, but they're also not afraid to showcase their personality and speak in front of a camera."

Growing and Maintaining Your Brand Beyond College

Raymond says because top college athletes make so much money from collective deals, they don't prioritize their social media. It's a big mistake, he says, because it means the money stops flowing as soon as you aren't playing.

"There's a lot of them that are leaving tons of money and opportunities on the table, not only to make more money, but also to build relationships with companies like Gatorade, TurboTax, Nike, Dick's Sporting Goods, Champs, and the like. Where, if they really took it seriously, they could be like an Alyssa Ustby, or Brevin Galloway, or Meechie Johnson, and do ten to twenty different brand deals throughout their college career, make an extra $200,000, $300,000 $400,000, and then on top of it, get paid by collective and then go off to be a pro and have a lot of great relationships with great companies like that."

Cole has continued working with Raymond after graduation. "They've been instrumental in helping me transition from collegiate athletics to building my personal brand outside of Duke track-and-field. This new phase has been challenging for sure but super exciting, and I'm grateful to still have the community I built while a student-athlete, just with more time to invest in connecting with them now that I'm no longer balancing classes."

Content Strategy

Glover said she's kept some consistency in her content post-graduation because she still talks about volleyball thanks to her broadcasting opportunities and does features like day-in-the-life content. "I think those help transition my audience so my content isn't entirely different. They're just following me now in a different part of my life."

"Alex Glover is a great example. She repurposes her old *Day in the Life as a D1 Volleyball Player* videos by turning them into a throwback series. Alex also gave her content a fresh spin by flipping her series into *Day in the Life of a Washed-Up D1 Volleyball Player*.

It's a perfect example of how to transition your content while staying true to your audience and maintaining engagement," said Green.

Green says by reimagining old footage and creatively framing your new reality, you can keep your audience entertained and invested in your journey, even after your athletic career ends.

"My content has naturally evolved from showcasing my life as a student-athlete at Duke to sharing the lessons and insights I've gained from that chapter, all while documenting my journey as I work toward professional running," said Cole. "Mainly, I've been more intentional about offering value-driven content that resonates with my audience. This ranges from being vulnerable about my own struggles, like finishing my collegiate career feeling injured and burned out, and the process of rebuilding my health and confidence after graduation, to more broad topics like figuring out who I want to be and how I want to spend my time for the rest of my life."

Cole has also started a new podcast with her sister, country music singer Julia Cole, called *Hustle & Harmony*. "Having the podcast with my sister Julia has really helped me expand my messaging, and I've even brought on team members to help with marketing and editing, which has made it so much easier to consistently share posts about my life, yes, but more so the themes in *The Players' Plate* that I'm so passionate about sharing to more athletes. I'm trying to show people the balance of chasing big dreams while taking care of yourself – and sharing that journey authentically has been a big part of my growth on social media."

It's never too soon to start approaching your social media strategically. You'll have a much easier time transitioning after graduation if you put some thought into your content before that day comes.

"I encourage my athletes to start bridging their social media content to reflect their life beyond sports," said Green. "By incorporating hints, teases, or showcases of their future plans, they can build an audience that connects with them beyond the roster."

Growing and Maintaining Your Brand Beyond College

Green gives a great example:

If one of my athletes wants to become a nurse but also land brand deals, I encourage them to feature their clinical hours as part of a "day-in-the-life" series while still a student-athlete. This helps their audience fall in love with who they are as a person – not just as an athlete. You can feature cute scrubs and tag the brand, or showcase the hair gel you use to slick your hair back before a shift at the hospital. Focus on products that fit seamlessly into your daily life and career aspirations. This approach keeps your audience engaged while paving the way for future partnerships.

Bassitt says the most important thing is to be yourself. "People can tell when you aren't being true to yourself on social media or in your posts. Don't take a deal just because of the money attached to it; make sure the deal and the company are something you're comfortable representing and are a good representation of what you value."

Cole agrees, saying brands are drawn to people who stand for something and are living authentically. "Whether through social media, speaking engagements, or creating something entirely new, like a business or podcast, staying true to your passions and showing how you're making an impact beyond the sport makes all the difference."

Back in Chapter 2, you also learned about Memphis thrower Riley Simmons, who has been working on building her public speaking experience. As Green explains:

No matter what an athlete wants to do after graduation, leveraging their name on the roster can help pave the way. Simmons aspires to be a motivational speaker, so I helped her create content that aligns with that goal. She shared clips of herself speaking at local high schools, used motivational audio overlays on her training videos, and even organized a sports camp for local kids.

NIL is about more than just brand deals – it's about using the platform you have to build something bigger. By showcasing her speaking skills and community impact, Simmons is laying the foundation for her future career while still capitalizing on her current visibility as a student-athlete.

Chapters 3 and 4 emphasized highlighting your hobbies and interests, and even your career aspirations, in your content. Not only does that allow niche brands to find you, but it also sets you up for life after your time as an athlete.

Building Lasting Relationships

Graduating doesn't mean you have to stop working with the brands you connected with in college. According to Green, "Many successful influencers make a living through brand deals, and you can do the same even after your athletic career ends. Start incorporating brands into your content that align with your next chapter."

Green says Laney Higgins (detailed in Chapter 2) is a great example of creating a long-term partnership with a brand. "She created a content series called W4lking and T4lking, where she interviews female athletes on their way to class. Laney became the first collegiate athlete signed by Lululemon because they saw the potential in her series and invested in it. Now, every episode features Lululemon branding, giving the brand recurring exposure and value over multiple videos – not just a one-off post."

Integrating the brand into her series puts Higgins in a strong position to continue to work with Lululemon long-term. "This approach not only maximizes the partnership's impact but also opens the door for long-term collaboration. What's stopping Lululemon from continuing to support W4lking and T4lking after Laney graduates? Nothing! Even after graduation, Laney can keep interviewing collegiate athletes and continue partnering with Lululemon, proving that athletes can remain relevant and valuable content creators beyond their sports careers."

Syd McKinney, former Wichita State and current professional softball athlete featured for her art in Chapter 2, says NIL opportunities have been a little more limited for her since graduating, but that the ones she does have are more than just one-off earning opportunities. "While I am a professional athlete, softball still has a long way to go in the professional space, which I think has impacted deals. However, I do think my current deals are more meaningful post-college, as I have built great relationships with the brands I work with."

If you want to maintain long-term partnerships, Green advises that you focus first and foremost on offering long-term value to your brand partners.

Making Connections

Another benefit of NIL is the opportunity to make connections for your career after graduation. Anna Camden is a prime example, mentioned back in the introduction. Both Camden and Glover took advantage of opportunities to hone their broadcasting skills while competing as college athletes, and both made important connections they could call on to start and grow their careers as broadcasters.

Mo Hasan, a former Vanderbilt and USC quarterback who went on to sign with the Tennessee Titans, has never been solely focused on football. In addition to founding nonprofit Second Spoon during his time at Vanderbilt that followed him out to USC, he also started a podcast (discussed in Chapter 2).

The benefits of the *Momentum Podcast* have gone far beyond simple monetization for Hasan, however. "After college, *Momentum* has helped me connect with tons of people that I likely would not have met otherwise – either as guests, executives of networks, brands, and so on. As other media entities have taken notice of our clips on Instagram and TikTok, some have offered jobs and other paid opportunities under their network."

Since graduating, Cole has found the time to focus more on connecting, especially in person. "I've started hosting group runs and it's been a super rewarding process to meet new friends and share my love for running, as well as create a great opportunity for new brands to support me helping get more people moving and inspired to chase their dreams in this next chapter of my life."

Her best advice for growing your network in meaningful ways? "Treat every partnership like it's a big deal, even the smaller ones, because you never know where a connection might lead. Being professional, following up, and finding ways to overdeliver opens so many doors you might not have even imagined as options beforehand."

Key Takeaways

- Start planning for post-college before you graduate. Begin bridging your content to reflect your future plans while still in college to create a smooth transition for your audience and brand partners.
- Developing a strong social media following during your college career sets you up for continued opportunities after graduation, especially if you won't be playing professionally.

(continued)

Growing and Maintaining Your Brand Beyond College

(continued)

- Share insights, experiences, and lessons learned rather than just documenting your athletic career to maintain audience engagement after graduation.
- Use NIL opportunities to build professional connections. The relationships you develop through brand partnerships, podcasts, and other content creation can lead to career opportunities beyond sports.
- After college, many athletes shift from performance-focused content to broader lifestyle content that appeals to their established audience.

Chapter 11

The Future of NIL and Revenue Sharing in College Sports

At the time of this writing, NIL is four years old. In those four years, we've seen huge shifts in how the NCAA, institutions, state legislatures, and high school sports associations have approached this growing market.

In an effort to give you a guide that won't be obsolete any time soon, the majority of this volume has focused on things that won't change, such as the importance of building a personal brand, protecting your intellectual property, and avoiding shady agents, vague or overreaching contracts, and those types of things.

In this chapter, however, there's some prognostication and analysis of things to come. Updates will be made available when necessary at https://www.athletesnilplaybook.com/updates.

The Future of NIL

The ability of college athletes to monetize their name, image, and likeness isn't going anywhere, and high school is increasingly trending in the same direction. Expectations are that NIL rules will only expand or loosen, not contract.

What is changing however, is institutional involvement. Really, this has been changing since NIL began. In the early months, schools had lengthy lists of what athletes couldn't do, from working with competitors to athlete department sponsors to using school names or logos in commercial content. Most athletic departments didn't even feel comfortable introducing a current sponsor to an athlete.

Most of those walls have come down, although it varies a little from school to school. The year 2025 will usher in what's expected to be wide-ranging support from athletic departments moving forward.

Increased Institutional Involvement

The states of Virginia and Georgia passed state laws in 2024 that allowed direct payments from universities to athletes, something that was against both the NCAA's rules (along with the NJCAA and NAIA) and many other state laws. Ohio followed with an executive order from the governor in late 2024.

The moves made it clear that the next frontier for athlete compensation is direct payments from universities to athletes for use of their NIL (in broadcasts, promotional materials, etc.). However, schools held off on taking advantage of these laws, likely a combination of the conflict with NCAA rules and the impending settlement in the *House v. NCAA* case, which would usher in a new era of revenue sharing with athletes.

Revenue Sharing

The settlement proposed in 2024 in the *House v. NCAA* case is poised to fundamentally alter the financial relationship between universities and their athletes, introducing direct revenue sharing for the first time in the history of college sports at the Division I level.

The case was initially filed by Grant House, a former Arizona State swimmer, former TCU women's basketball player Sedona Prince, and former Illinois football player Tamir Oliver, against the NCAA and the Power 5 conferences (Big Ten, Big 12, ACC, Pac-12, and SEC). The athletes were seeking compensation for lost NIL opportunities that predated the NCAA's rules change and alleging that the NCAA and Power 5 conferences had colluded to restrict athletes' earning potential.

A settlement was announced in July 2024 and also included two other cases (known as the *Carter* and *Hubbard* cases). Included in the settlement was back pay to former college athletes and a new framework to allow revenue sharing with athletes going forward.

Back Pay Provisions

The settlement included a substantial $2.8 billion in back pay to compensate athletes for lost opportunities between June 15, 2016, and September 15, 2024 (dates ultimately chosen by the court).

The distribution plan for this compensation would be based on various factors, including the athlete's sport, school, and years of participation. Proposed allocations detailed by the attorneys in the case were as follows:

- Football and men's basketball: $135,000 on average
- Women's basketball: $35,000 on average
- Others: dependent on the sport, school, years played and number of athletes who participate in the settlement
- Athletes who played in any Division I sport before the NCAA changed its rules in 2021 to allow for NIL will be eligible for additional compensation based on the NIL payments they received after the rule change. The highest damages in this category are expected to exceed $1 million, with the highest being estimated at $1.859 million.
- Athletes who played any Division I sport in a Power 5 between the 2019–20 and 2021–22 years will be eligible for thousands more to compensate for Alston awards (payments to athletes

from athletic departments allowed as a result of the *NCAA v. Alston* case for education-related expenses up to $5,980 per athlete, per year).[1]

There are three groups of athletes who will receive back pay under the settlement:

- **Football and men's basketball** athletes who received, or will receive, a full grant-in-aid scholarship and played, or will play, on a Division I men's basketball team or an FBS football team that is a member of the Power 5 (including Notre Dame) and have been, or will be, initially eligible from June 15, 2016, to September 15, 2024. Plaintiffs counsel Hagens Berman provided the following estimates for this group, broken down by the type of damages claimed:
  - Broadcast NIL: Average approx. $91,000. Range from $15,000 to $280,000.
  - Video game: Range from approx. $300 to $4,000 per athlete.
  - Lost NIL Opportunities: Average approx. $17,000. Range from less than $1 to approx. $800,000.
  - Pay-for-play: Average approx. $40,000.

- **Women's basketball** athletes who received, or will receive, a full grant-in-aid scholarship and played, or will play, on a Division I women's basketball team that is a member of the Power 5 (including Notre Dame) and have been, or will be, initially eligible from June 15, 2016, to September 15, 2024. Plaintiffs counsel Hagens Berman provided the following estimates for this group, broken down by the type of damages claimed:
  - Broadcast NIL: Average approx. $23,000. Range from $3,000 to $52,000.

- Lost NIL Opportunities: Average approx. $8,500. Range from less than $1 to $300,000.

- Pay-for-play: Average approx. $14,000.

- **All other athletes who played, or will play, on a Division I team** (other than those listed above, including football and basketball players in non-Power 5 conferences) and have been, or will be, initially eligible from June 15, 2016, to September 15, 2024. Plaintiffs counsel Hagens Berman provided the following estimates for this group:

  - Video game
    - Football and men's basketball in non-Power 5 conferences for video game: Range from approx. $300 to $4,000.

  - Pay-for-play
    - Baseball (Power 5): $400 average
    - Football, "Top Non-Power 5 Football" (AAC, Mountain West and BYU): $1,400 average
    - Men's Basketball, Big East: $6,700 average
    - Men's Basketball, "Top Non-Power 5" (AAC, Atlantic 10, Mountain West, Gonzaga): $2,400 average
    - Women's Basketball, "Top Non-Power 5" (AAC, Big East, Gonzaga): $300 average
    - All others: $50 average

  - Lost NIL opportunities
    - Average approx. $5,300. Range from less than $1 to $1,859,000.

Backpay payments will be made in equal, annual installments over ten years, with the first payment being made into the escrow account for distribution on May 15, 2025 (or within 45 days of the final order, whichever is later). In subsequent years, payments will be deposited into the escrow account for disbursement on July 15 each year.

The back pay would be funded through two primary sources:

- $1.2 billion from current NCAA reserves
- $1.6 billion from future NCAA distributions over a 10-year period

However, this funding structure has been criticized by non-Power 5 schools. The plan was that Power 5 institutions would bear 40% of the future distribution reductions and the Group of Five schools would cover 17%, although the bulk of payouts would go to Power 5 athletes. Smaller schools and conferences expressed frustration they were bearing a disproportionate burden of the settlement's costs.

Revenue Sharing Model

The more transformative aspect of the settlement, however, is the establishment of a framework that will see universities sharing revenue with athletes beginning in the 2025–2026 academic year. Although the NCAA will change its rules under the terms of the settlement to allow for universities to make direct payments to athletes, any payment to athletes above what is permitted in the settlement (and existed prior to it, such as Alston payments) is still prohibited.

The settlement allows schools to share up to 22% of the average revenue of the Power 5, plus Notre Dame, for specific revenue streams with their athletes, including:

- Ticket sales (including suite licenses)
- Game guarantees
- Media rights deals
- NCAA and conference distributions

Notably excluded from the calculation are booster contributions, traditionally a significant revenue source for athletic departments.

The initial sharing cap was set at $20.5 million per school per year beginning in 2025, with projections suggesting it could reach $33 million by 2035.

Each individual school will determine their level of participation, with the ability to share any amount between zero and the annual cap. In addition, the average shared revenue will be recalculated every three years during the term of the settlement (10 years), with the second and third year of each three-year period being a 4% increase on the previous year. There are also provisions to allow recalculations for new broadcast agreements or other significant revenue changes.

So how much can you expect as an athlete? Many schools indicated they would distribute revenue sharing funds according to the following approximate breakdown:

- 75–85% to football
- 10–15% to men's basketball
- 10–15% to other sports

The rationale behind this distribution strategy is that it aligns with how revenue is generated. However, Title IX experts warn there may be future challenges to this based on the uneven application between sexes. The U.S. Department of Education has confirmed that Title IX rules apply to revenue sharing, but they declined to offer guidance on how schools should distribute money in order to stay in compliance. It will likely be a question before courts in the future.

Roster and Scholarship Changes

The settlement eliminated traditional scholarship limits in favor of roster caps, allowing schools to offer full scholarships to every athlete on a roster. As part of this, roster sizes were increased beyond previous scholarship limits for virtually every sport, leading current athletes and recruits to believe it would create more scholarship opportunities.

However, this change doesn't mean teams will add to their current rosters or that more scholarships will be offered going forward. Each school will have the option – not the obligation – to increase rosters and award offerings.

Early indicators suggest that some schools might instead reduce overall athletic opportunities to fund revenue sharing, with estimates suggesting the elimination of approximately 3,000 roster positions.[2]

The new roster sizes are as follows:

- Acrobatics and Tumbling: 55
- Baseball: 34
- Basketball (men's): 15
- Basketball (women's): 15
- Beach Volleyball (women's): 19
- Bowling (women's): 11
- Cross Country (men's): 17
- Cross Country (women's): 17
- Equestrian (women's): 50
- Fencing (men's): 24
- Fencing (women's): 24
- Field Hockey (women's): 27
- Football: 105
- Golf (men's): 9
- Golf (women's): 9

- Gymnastics (men's): 20
- Gymnastics (women's): 20
- Ice Hockey (men's): 26
- Ice Hockey (women's): 26
- Indoor Track and Field (men's): 45
- Indoor Track and Field (women's): 45
- Lacrosse (men's): 48
- Lacrosse (women's): 38
- Outdoor Track and Field (men's): 45
- Outdoor Track and Field (women's): 45
- Rifle (12)
- Rowing (women's): 68
- Rugby (women's): 36
- Skiing (men's): 16
- Skiing (women's): 16
- Soccer (men's): 28
- Soccer (women's): 28
- Softball: 25
- Stunt: 65
- Swimming & Diving (men's): 30
- Swimming & Diving (women's): 30
- Tennis (men's): 10
- Tennis (women's): 10
- Triathlon (women's): 14
- Volleyball (men's): 18

The Future of NIL and Revenue Sharing in College Sports

- Volleyball (women's): 18

- Water Polo (men's): 24

- Water Polo (women's): 24

- Wrestling (men's): 30

- Wrestling (women's): 30

Unfortunately, some athletes were impacted almost immediately following the announcement of the settlement. By late 2024, more than a dozen parents of current college athletes or recruits had spoken with Yahoo! Sports about how the proposed settlement was already causing athletes to lose opportunities.

A Big 12 beach volleyball recruit who had been committed to a program for months was told her roster position no longer existed, while a sophomore cross country runner on an SEC team was notified she was cut from the team just two days after the Fall 2024 semester began. Another program in a power conference released all of their 2025 commitments for men's swimming. The settlement is also expected to eliminate more than 1,500 walk-on football players.[3]

New Financial Aid and Revenue Sharing Agreements

The traditional National Letter of Intent system is being replaced thanks to the *House* settlement. Instead, athletes will be offered financial aid contracts, which may include revenue sharing or may handle it in a separate document. It also means athletes are no longer signing to commit to a program for at least a year, as was the case with the NLI.

Revenue sharing won't come without conditions or strings attached. This book is being written as those contracts are being developed in anticipation of the *House* settlement ultimately being approved in 2025.

Some of the provisions being included in draft contracts reviewed for this book, and by attorneys who weighed in as part of this chapter, included:

- Payouts incrementally during the season that end if an athlete decides to transfer, is ruled ineligible, or is no longer on the active roster
- Buyout clauses similar to those found in coaching contracts where amounts already received must be repaid
- Increasing or decreasing the amount based on academic benchmarks
- Financial penalties for team rule violations or criminal charges
- Requirements for athletes to serve as university ambassadors and create content, make appearances, etc. for the university or its partners
- Waiving future claims that the athlete is an employee or that a coach's decision impacted the athlete's NIL value

Transfer Portal Restrictions

Attorney Ryan Mulvaney says he's reviewed Memorandums of Understanding (MOUs) that attempt to prevent athletes from entering the transfer portal. "College athletes are entitled to exercise their discretion to enter the NCAA Transfer Portal," he says. "Correspondingly, some MOUs that do not attempt to restrict college athletes from entering the NCAA Transfer Portal nevertheless attempt to claw back monies paid to college athletes if those athletes enter the portal. Language should be included to strategically structure the payments due to the athlete or to limit the extent of the claw back of monies."

Compensation Reductions and Termination

Among the issues attorneys are flagging in agreements are sweeping clauses that allow for compensation to be adjusted.

Attorney Heitner says a contract he reviewed, which is based on the Big Ten's template, read (in bold type): "The Institution in its discretion may, at any time, adjust the Consideration to reflect an increase or decrease in the Athlete's NIL value (e.g., a Heisman Trophy win may increase the NIL value and reduced playing time may decrease the NIL value)."[4]

Athletes have no reason to agree to a contract that allows a collective, athletic department, or university to reduce compensation or terminate the contract at their discretion or "without cause." Reductions and terminations should be allowed only under specifics laid out in the contract that you understand and have agreed to in advance.

On the flipside, it begs the question whether there should be escalators, or other potential for increases, when an athlete performs beyond expectations or forgoes other offers to stay at an institution.

Mulvaney says he's seen MOUs that permit the university to terminate if the athlete is convicted of, or pleads guilty to, any criminal offenses, enters the transfer portal, or violates any morality clauses or the rules and policies of the university, conference, or NCAA.

"I have seen some MOUs that even attempt to allow universities to terminate upon the change of head coaches."

The most important thing to understand and negotiate for here is what happens to the money paid to an athlete if the MOU is terminated. "Language should be included to protect the athlete's claim to those monies and any monies earned before termination," says Mulvaney.

Morality Clauses

Mulvaney says another clause athletes need to pay special attention to is a morals clause, which is standard in the Uniform Player Contracts in professional leagues. These clauses allow the university to terminate if athletes engage in unlawful conduct that could harm the reputation of the university or that could offend community standards.

"Such conduct could include engaging in activities related to drugs, alcohol abuse, sexual misconduct, illegal gambling, and being convicted of felonies," he said.

Waiver Clauses

Waiver clauses are being included in some contracts where athletes are waiving future legal claims against the university or coaches.

"Some MOUs might attempt to require athletes to waive claims against the universities for what I refer to as 'coaches' decisions,' namely playing time and a lack thereof, and decisions impacting athletes' roles, performance, or prohibiting athletes from participating in games. Those provisions usually also require athletes to waive claims that such 'coaches' decisions' impacted negatively the athlete's NIL value."

Mulvaney says some schools might even attempt including waiver clauses that cover future employment claims by athletes.

How these agreements are being negotiated and managed differs from school to school. Some have already hired general managers or have created new departments to manage NIL and revenue sharing, including salary cap management, negotiations, compliance, payments, and more.

It's expected coaches will be allotted an amount for their team and then given the discretion – along with their staff, which increasingly includes a football-specific general manager – to determine how funds will be distributed across the team.

It's important to note that athletes will still be able to earn from NIL deals above and beyond revenue sharing. For example, an athlete might receive a revenue sharing amount from the athletic department and also earn additional income through NIL deals procured through a collective, agent/agency, marketplace, or direct from brands.

Ongoing Legal Challenges

You didn't sign up for a law class, so you won't be getting one here. However, alongside NIL and revenue sharing, efforts to classify at least some athletes as employees could change the future of athlete compensation.

From antitrust lawsuits not resolved with the *House* case to petitions filed with the National Labor Relations Board, there are myriad ways athlete compensation could be altered going forward.

You can track ongoing legal challenges in college sports at https://www.athletesnilplaybook.com/legalchallenges.

Key Takeaways

- The ability for athletes to monetize their name, image, and likeness isn't going away, and rules are more likely to broaden than contract in the future.
- The *House v. NCAA* settlement establishes a framework allowing universities to share up to 22% of specific revenue streams with athletes, with caps starting at $20.5 million per school per year in 2025.
- Revenue sharing won't replace NIL deals. Athletes will still be able to earn from brand partnerships, collectives, and other NIL opportunities beyond what they receive through revenue sharing agreements with their universities.
- The traditional National Letter of Intent system is being replaced with financial aid contracts that may include revenue sharing terms and conditions.

- Revenue sharing contracts may include provisions like incremental payments, buyout clauses, academic benchmarks, transfer restrictions, and morality clauses that could affect payment.
- Many agreements include clauses allowing universities to reduce compensation or terminate contracts under specific circumstances, potentially requiring repayment of previously received funds.
- Alongside NIL and revenue sharing developments, ongoing legal actions seek to classify some athletes as employees, which could further transform athlete compensation in the future.

Conclusion

Within these pages, I've attempted to arm you with the knowledge you need to define, grow, and monetize your personal brand. Your time as an athlete won't last forever, but you can use the platform it provides you to set yourself up for everything that comes after it.

By all means, monetize your NIL. Don't make that your only focus, though. Use NIL as a way to network, grow your skills, and discover what you enjoy doing outside of playing your sport.

And don't forget to protect yourself! It can sound expensive and time-consuming to consult with an attorney, but many offer free consults or offer very low fees to college athletes. If you have a law school on your campus, they might even offer free contract review. The little bit of time and money you'll spend at this stage can save you a great deal of money and frustration in the future.

Athletes, I can't wait to see what you do with your NIL, and I hope you'll reach out and tell me about it.

Parents, please join me in my Facebook group where you can ask your NIL questions and get feedback from experts: www.facebook.com/groups/parentsnilplaybook.

Good luck!

Acknowledgments

Dear reader, thank you for spending some time with me. I don't at all take for granted the time or money you spent on this book.

I first started writing about name, image, and likeness during the *O'Bannon* trial, so this is a bit of a full-circle moment for me. I've been wanting to write this book since NIL began, but it felt like things would never slow down and stop changing enough for me to be able to write something that would stay current.

As I began outlining this book, I knew I wanted to represent a variety of athlete experiences with NIL to show the athletes coming up behind them that NIL is something everyone can pursue. So, first and foremost, thank you to the following athletes who participated: Josh Africa, Trevor Bassitt, Jack Betts, General Booty, Anna Camden, Leah Clapper, Emily Cole, Alex Glover. Chase Griffin, Emma Halter, Mo Hasan, Laney Higgins, Shani Idlette, Ra-Sun Kazadi, Reese Lechner, Keshawn Lynch, Syd McKiney, Chloe Mitchell, Riley Simmons, Rayquan Smith, and Cate Urbani. Also a big thank-you to Tikisha Gobourne and Hannah Lechner for sharing their experiences as parents helping their athletes navigate this space.

Many professionals graciously gave of their time and expertise for this book as well, including Christian Addison, Dorie Clark, Sean Ellenby, Caroline Frazier, Joshua Frieser, Josh Gerben, Sam Green, Darren Heitner, Brittany Hennessy, Maribeth Kuzbeski, Blake Lawrence, Marty Ludwig, Ksenia Maiorova, Amy Maldonado,

233

Daniel Marks, Ryan Mulvaney, Michael Raymond, Carl Spencer, Andy Vodopia, Becca Wathen, and Cody Wilcoxson.

A big thank-you to the parents who read early drafts and gave me notes that made this book stronger: Tara Clapper, Bre Jones, Destinee Jordan, and Hannah Lechner. You ladies are the best!

Two of my former students also helped with projects surrounding this book. A big thank-you to Logan Vild and Presleigh Liss.

This book wouldn't be in your hands without the belief of Zach Schisgal at Wiley. Thank you, Zach, for everything you did to help bring this book to market!

My husband, Chadd, was a big support throughout this process, whether he was making me dinner while I wrote, ignoring messes I created, listening to me vent, or just helping me stay motivated. Love on!

My family let me work on this book on Christmas Eve and Christmas to meet my deadline, so a big thank-you to my supportive mother, father, brother, sister-in-law, and very patient nieces. I have the best extended family in the world, so lots of love to all my aunts, uncles, and cousins who always support my dreams!

Last but not least, to my incredible friends and colleagues in the college sports industry. Thank you for sharing my articles, inviting me to speak, and otherwise helping promote me and my work.

About the Author

Kristi Dosh is a former practicing attorney who is now a sports business contributor for *Forbes* and the founder of Business of College Sports®. She has written on the business of college sports for more than a decade for outlets such as ESPN, *The Washington Post,* and *Sports Business Journal.*

In addition to her reporting, Kristi is the author of another book on the business of college sports: *Saturday Millionaires: How Winning Football Builds Winning Colleges.* She is also a consultant for athletic departments, universities, and NIL collectives on matters ranging from strategic planning to conference realignment and navigating the new name, image, and likeness landscape.

Currently, Kristi teaches courses at the University of Florida on NIL in the sport management and public relations departments, and in the law school, in addition to College Sports Reporting and Sports Media Law and Ethics in the journalism department. She has hosted two NIL podcasts: *Game Face* from Linktree and *The Players' Platform* with former Duke track and field athlete Emily Cole.

Kristi lives on Amelia Island in Florida with her husband, German shepherd, and three cats. She holds a BA from Oglethorpe University and a JD from the University of Florida.

Notes

Chapter 1

1. Putterman, Alex. "UCF Kicker Ruled Ineligible After Failing to Agree to NCAA Conditions on His YouTube Videos." The Comeback, August 1, 2017. https://thecomeback.com/ncaa/ucf-kicker-ruled-ineligible-failing-agree-ncaa-conditions-youtube-videos.html.
2. Kopet, Adam. "Texas A&M Freshman Ryan Trahan Granted NCAA Waiver to Compete and Operate His Business." RunnerSpace.com, September 22, 2017. https://www.runnerspace.com/news.php?news_id=492443.
3. Thompson, Jackson. "The NCAA Cut Former NFL Player Jeremy Bloom's College Football Career Short. Now He's Fighting to Get College Athletes Endorsement Rights." Business Insider, June 12, 2021. https://www.businessinsider.com/nfl-ncaa-jeremy-bloom-documentary-student-athletes-2021-6.
4. Trahan, Kevin. "Explaining the NCAA V. O'Bannon College Athletics Case." Vox, June 2, 2014. https://www.vox.com/2014/6/2/5772266/explaining-the-ncaa-v-obannon-college-athletics-case.
5. Berkowitz, Steve, and Christine Brennan. "Justice Department Warns NCAA Over Transfer and Name, Image, Likeness Rules." *USA Today*, January 8, 2021. https://www.usatoday.com/story/sports/ncaaf/2021/01/08/justice-department-warns-ncaa-over-transfer-and-money-making-rules/6599747002/.
6. Dosh, Kristi. "With NCAA Stepping Back from NIL Regulations, Colleges Begin Preparing to Adopt Their Own Policies." *Forbes*, June 25, 2021. https://www.forbes.com/sites/kristidosh/2021/06/24/schools-begin-preparing-to-adopt-their-own-nil-policies/.

7. Dosh, Kristi. interview with Ksenia Maiorova and Amy Maldonado, *Business of College Sports* podcast, February 2, 2023. https://business ofcollegesports.com/name-image-likeness/new-developments-in-nil-for-international-student-athletes/.

8. Dosh, Kristi. "New Developments in NIL for International Student Athletes." Business of College Sports, March 17, 2023. https://businessof collegesports.com/name-image-likeness/new-developments-in-nil-for-international-student-athletes/.

9. Maiorova, Ksenia, and Amy Maldonado. *NIL X Immigration: A practical guide to NIL for international student-athletes, collegiate athletic directors, NIL collectives, agencies, and other industry stakeholders,* 2023.

10. Zion, Brittany. "Kieron Van Wyk and ASE Representation: Pioneering NIL Exemptions for International Student-Athletes." Eccker Sports Group, July 18, 2024. https://ecckersports.com/industry-insights/kieron-van-wyk-and-ase-representation-pioneering-nil-exemptions-for-international-student-athletes/.

11. Darcey, Reed. "LSU's Last-Tear Poa breaking new ground with NIL lawsuit." *The Advocate*, November 13, 2024. https://www.nola.com/sports/lsu/lsu-womens-basketball-nil-lawsuit-last-tear-poa-zach-edey-oscar-tshiebwe/article_3d55970e-9bc2-11ef-a2a1-d3e61b3a1349.html.

12. Nakos, Pete. "Five-star Notre Dame OT Commit Will Black Missing Out on NIL Packages Due to Visa Restrictions." On3, August 19, 2024. https://www.on3.com/nil/news/five-star-notre-dame-offensive-tackle-commit-will-black-missing-out-on-nil-packages-due-to-visa-restrictions/.

13. Dosh, Kristi. interview with Ksenia Maiorova and Amy Maldonado, *Business of College Sports* podcast, February 2, 2023. https://business ofcollegesports.com/name-image-likeness/new-developments-in-nil-for-international-student-athletes/; and Dosh, Kristi, interview with Ksenia Maiorova and Amy Maldonado, *Business of College Sports* podcast, November 28, 2023. https://businessofcollegesports.com/name-image-likeness/nil-guidance-for-international-student-athletes-in-2023/.

14. Tucker, Kyle. "Kentucky's Oscar Tshiebwe Gets Down to NIL Business in the Bahamas." *The Athletic*, August 12, 2022. https://www.nytimes.com/athletic/3493805/2022/08/10/kentucky-oscar-tshiebwe-nil-bahamas/.

Chapter 2

1. Severin, Kevin. "OSU's Sanders Partners With Stillwater's Eskimo Joe's." KOKH, November 9, 2022. https://okcfox.com/sports/oklahoma-state-cowboys/spencer-sanders-stillwater-eskimo-joes-nil-deal-shirt-pete-joe-restaurant-autographs-proceeds.

2. Cohen, Kelly. "Georgia Bulldogs QB Stetson Bennett Surprises Customers at Raising Cane's Chicken Restaurant – ESPN." ESPN, January 14, 2022. https://www.espn.com/college-football/story/_/id/33061912/georgia-bulldogs-qb-stetson-bennett-surprises-customers-raising-cane-chicken-restaurant.

3. Dosh, Kristi. "Boost Mobile Seeing Positive ROI from Its NIL Program." *Forbes*, March 2, 2022. https://www.forbes.com/sites/kristidosh/2022/02/28/boost-mobile-seeing-positive-roi-from-its-nil-program/.

4. "NIL Store Athletes Surpass $1 Million in Payouts Article." NIL Store, January 18, 2024. https://nil.store/blogs/news/nil-store-surpasses-1-million-in-athlete-payouts.

5. Dosh, Kristi. "Tracker: Student Athlete Podcasts and Paid Guest Series." Business of College Sports, January 17, 2023. https://businessofcollegesports.com/tracker-student-athlete-podcasts-and-paid-guest-series/.

6. Clark, Dorie. "How Much Should You Charge for a Speech?" *Harvard Business Review*, October 24, 2020. https://hbr.org/2018/05/how-much-should-you-charge-for-a-speech.

7. Traylor, Grant. "New NIL Rules Are Music to Will Ulmer's Ears." *Herald-Dispatch*, July 1, 2021. https://www.herald-dispatch.com/sports/new-nil-rules-are-music-to-will-ulmers-ears/article_aa800e18-501a-5bf0-9723-5e07629edd21.html.

8. "New Heights: Gordon McKernan Teams Up with Flau'jae Johnson for Super Bowl Commercial Featuring Get Gordon Jingle Rap." Gordon McKernan Injury Attorneys, February 12, 2024. https://www.getgordon.com/blog/new-heights-gordon-mckernan-teams-up-with-flaujae-johnson-for-super-bowl-commercial-featuring-get-gordon-jingle-rap/.

9. Lyles, Harry, Jr. "How NIL Helped SMU Football's Ra'Sun Kazadi 'grow as an Artist' – ESPN." ESPN, July 3, 2022. https://www.espn.com/college-football/story/_/id/34014460/how-nil-helped-smu-football-rasun-kazadi-grow-artist.
10. Dosh, Kristi. "First NIL Car Deal With LSU's Myles Brennan Exposes Risk for Brands." Business of College Sports, September 4, 2021. https://businessofcollegesports.com/name-image-likeness/first-nil-car-deal-with-lsus-myles-brennan-exposes-risk-for-brands/.
11. Dosh, Kristi. "Utah Basketball Teams and Women's Gymnasts Receive New Cars in NIL Deal." Business of College Sports, December 14, 2023. https://businessofcollegesports.com/name-image-likeness/utah-basketball-teams-and-womens-gymnasts-receive-new-cars-in-nil-deal/.

Chapter 3

1. Kelly, Darian. "These College Athletes Have Landed NIL Deals With Their Dogs." *Business of College Sports*, January 10, 2025. https://businessofcollegesports.com/name-image-likeness/these-5-cfb-stars-and-their-dogs-have-landed-nil-partnerships/.

Chapter 4

1. Whitler, Kimberly A. "How Marketers Choose College Athlete Influencers." *Harvard Business Review*, April 10, 2024. https://hbr.org/2024/05/how-marketers-choose-college-athlete-influencers.
2. Weber, Sam. "NIL AT 3: The Annual Opendorse Report." Opendorse, August 5, 2024. https://biz.opendorse.com/blog/nil-3-opendorse-report/.

Chapter 5

1. NCAA.org. "Student-athletes Share Experiences With NIL at NCAA Convention." NCAA.org, January 13, 2024. https://www.ncaa.org/news/2024/1/11/media-center-student-athletes-share-experiences-with-nil-at-ncaa-convention.aspx.

2. Fleming, Margaret. "A TikToker and College Athlete Has Scored 86 NIL Deals in 2 Years. Read the Exact Email Templates He Uses to Cold-pitch Brands." *Business Insider*, October 3, 2023. https://www.businessinsider.com/student-athlete-nil-brand-deals-email-template-hbcu-football-track-2023-9.

Chapter 6

1. Mandel, Stewart, and Justin Williams. "The Unprecedented Million-dollar Recruitment of the Nation's Best Softball Player." *The Athletic*, July 30, 2024. https://www.nytimes.com/athletic/5664181/2024/07/29/nijaree-canady-texas-tech-nil-million-dollar-contract/.
2. X (formerly Twitter). https://x.com/MatthewSluka/status/1838799758577799607.
3. Christovich, Amanda. "Former FSU Basketball Players Sue Coach Over 'Broken' NIL Promises." Front Office Sports, December 30, 2024. https://frontofficesports.com/fsu-basket-ball-players-lawsuit-nil/.
4. Evans, Luca. "Is USC Prepared for NIL Floodgates Opening and No NCAA Restrictions?" *Daily News*, April 11, 2024. https://www.dailynews.com/2024/04/10/is-usc-prepared-for-nil-floodgates-opening-and-no-ncaa-restrictions/amp/.
5. Facebook. https://www.facebook.com/story.php/?story_fbid=913221134180607&id=100064781854436.
6. X (formerly Twitter). https://x.com/DarrenHeitner/status/1874158186204385412.
7. Portnoy, Ben. "Two Circles See Opportunities with NIL in Launching College Division." *SportsBusiness Journal*, June 4, 2024. https://www.sportsbusinessjournal.com/Articles/2024/06/04/two-circles.
8. McCann, Michael. "NFLer's Suit Draws Big League Advance Into NIL Pay Vortex." Sportico.com, September 6, 2023. https://www.sportico.com/law/analysis/2023/dexter-v-big-league-advance-lawsuit-1234736365/.
9. Murphy, Dan. "Nilly NIL Company Pay College Athletes Kendrick Perkins – ESPN." ESPN.Com, October 8, 2024. https://www.espn.com/college-sports/story/_/id/41664466/nilly-nil-company-college-athletes-kendrick-perkins-consumer-protection-experts.

Chapter 7

1. Heitner, Darren. "Newsletter, Image, Likeness Vol. 102: Diego Pavia Provides a Lesson About Group Licensing Deals," October 18, 2024. https://www.linkedin.com/pulse/newsletter-image-likeness-vol-102-diego-pavia-provides-darren-heitner-wkk1e/.

2. Smith, Michael. "OneTeam, Fanatics Building Major College Group Licensing Business, but 'Nobody Is Getting Rich Off Jerseys.'" *SportsBusiness Journal*, January 30, 2023. https://www.sportsbusinessjournal.com/Journal/Issues/2023/01/30/Upfront/collegiate-licensing.aspx.

3. Christovich, Amanda. "Athletes Are Receiving Below-Market Cut of Fanatics CFB Jerseys." Front Office Sports, September 9, 2022. https://frontofficesports.com/below-market-rate-fanatics-cfb/.

4. Fleming, Margaret. "Vanderbilt QB Disputes Licensed NIL Apparel: 'This Is Not Me.'" Front Office Sports, October 15, 2024. https://frontofficesports.com/diego-pavia-vanderbilt-t-shirt-dispute-turnt/.

5. Rothenberg, Jack. "Upper Deck President Jason Masherah Discusses Brand's Approach to NIL Partnerships." Business of College Sports, December 8, 2022. https://businessofcollegesports.com/name-image-likeness/upper-deck-president-jason-masherah-discusses-brands-approach-to-nil-partnerships/.

6. Saul, Derek. "Fanatics Inks Historic College Trading Card Deal – And Some Athletes Will Get Their Due." *Forbes*, June 10, 2022. https://www.forbes.com/sites/dereksaul/2022/06/09/fanatics-inks-historic-college-trading-card-deal-and-some-athletes-will-get-their-due/.

7. Crosby, Robert. "Georgia Football QB JT Daniels Signs Major NIL Deal." *Sports Illustrated*, August 16, 2021. https://www.si.com/college/georgia/news/georgia-football-jt-daniels-nil-deal.

8. Boise State University Athletics. "Boise State and Jacksons Announce Exclusive Football Trading Cards," BroncoSports.com, October 5, 2022. https://broncosports.com/news/2022/10/5/boise-state-and-jacksons-announce-exclusive-football-trading-cards.

9. Jones, Brandon. "Introducing TexAgs NIL Trading Cards Featuring A&M Student-athletes," TexAgs.com, September 9, 2022. https://texags.com/s/46972/introducing-texags-nil-trading-cards-featuring-am-student-athletes.

10. Ehrlich, Michael. "LSU Gymnastics Star Elena Arenas Launches Her First NIL Trading Card – Sports Illustrated NIL on FanNation News, Analysis and More." *Sports Illustrated*, November 26, 2023. https://www.si.com/fannation/name-image-likeness/news/lsu-gymnast-launches-her-first-trading-card-michael9.

11. Mezzy, Caleb. "NIL's Impact on the Trading Card Industry: The Opportunities, Challenges and Potential Value." *The Athletic*, December 20, 2024. https://www.nytimes.com/athletic/6007159/2024/12/19/nil-sports-cards-ncaa/.

12. Brown, Matt. "How ONIT Is Trying to Make College Athlete Trading Cards Work." Extra Points, March 14, 2024. https://www.extrapointsmb.com/p/onit-trying-make-college-athlete-trading-cards-work.

13. Rissinger, Hailey. "Latest Updates on EA Sports College Football 25 Release." Business of College Sports, December 25, 2024. https://businessofcollegesports.com/marketingpr/ea-sports-provides-update-on-upcoming-video-game/.

14. Dosh, Kristi. "What's in the EA Sports College Football Contract?" Business of College Sports, February 23, 2024. https://businessofcollegesports.com/name-image-likeness/whats-in-the-ea-sports-college-football-contract/.

15. Dosh, Kristi. "Subscription Box for UNC Tarheel Fans Latest Creative NIL Idea." Business of College Sports, February 24, 2022. https://businessofcollegesports.com/name-image-likeness/subscription-box-for-unc-tarheel-fans-latest-creative-nil-idea/.

16. "Taco Bell Case Study." The Brandr Group. https://thebrandrgroup.com/case-study/taco-bell-case-study/.

17. Dosh, Kristi. "Group Licensing Opportunities Continue to Grow for Student Athletes." *Forbes*, May 22, 2023. https://www.forbes.com/sites/kristidosh/2023/05/19/group-licensing-opportunities-continue-to-grow-for-student-athletes/.

18. Lev, Jacob, and Amy Woodyatt. "Florida Gators Quarterback Anthony Richardson Will No Longer Use 'AR15' Nickname for This Reason," CNN. https://www.cnn.com/2022/07/18/sport/anthony-richardson-ar-15-gun-violence-intl-spt/index.html.

19. Townsend, Brad. "Luka Doncic, Mom Quietly Settle Trademark Dispute." *Dallas News*, January 10, 2023. https://www.dallasnews.com/sports/mavericks/2023/01/05/mavericks-star-luka-doncic-and-his-mother-have-quietly-settled-trademark-dispute/.

Chapter 8

1. Bonagura, Kyle. "Top College Football Prospect T.A. Cunningham Ruled Eligible to Play for California High School After Weekslong Transfer Drama." ESPN.com, September 26, 2022. https://www.espn.com/college-football/story/_/id/34671021/top-college-football-prospect-ta-cunningham-ruled-eligible-play-california-high-school-weeks-long-transfer-drama.

2. Mandel, Stewart, Bruce Feldman, and Andy Staples. "How a Five-star Prospect from Georgia Ended Up Homeless, Ineligible and 2,000 Miles Away." *The Athletic*, September 19, 2022. https://www.nytimes.com/athletic/3605831/2022/09/19/t-a-cunningham-eligibility-recruiting-nil/.

3. Bonagura, "Top College Football Prospect T.A. Cunningham Ruled Eligible to Play for California High School After Weekslong Transfer Drama."

4. Dosh, Kristi. "Chase Griffin on Launching the Athlete's Bureau." Business of College Sports, January 19, 2024. https://businessofcollegesports.com/name-image-likeness/chase-griffin-on-launching-the-athletes-bureau/.

5. "Fanatics Refiles Lawsuit Against Cardinals' Rookie Marvin Harrison Jr." FOX 10 Phoenix, August 26, 2024. https://www.fox10phoenix.com/sports/fanatics-refiles-lawsuit-against-cardinals-rookie-marvin-harrison-jr.

6. Roeloffs, Mary Whitfill. "Buccaneers Quarterback Baker Mayfield Sues Family for Alleged $12 Million Theft." *Forbes*, December 2, 2024. https://www.forbes.com/sites/maryroeloffs/2024/11/26/buccaneers-quarterback-baker-mayfield-sues-family-for-alleged-12-million-theft/.
7. Badenhausen, Kurt. "Parents Blow Tennis Star's $60 Million Fortune." *Forbes*, February 8, 2012. https://www.forbes.com/sites/kurtbadenhausen/2012/02/08/parents-blow-tennis-stars-60-million-fortune/.

Chapter 9

1. Butler, Sarah Lorge. "Six-Time NCAA Champion Parker Valby Signs With New Balance." *Runner's World*, October 17, 2024. https://www.runnersworld.com/news/a62548221/parker-valby-signs-with-new-balance/.

Chapter 11

1. "Hagens Berman and Winston & Strawn Seek Court Approval of Historic Settlement to Revolutionize College Sports," June 22, 2021. https://www.hbsslaw.com/press/ncaa-student-athlete-name-image-and-likeness/hagens-berman-and-winston-strawn-seek-court-approval-of-historic-settlement-to-revolutionize-college-sports.
2. Dellenger, Ross. "Historic House-NCAA settlement Leaving Hundreds of Olympic Sport Athletes in Peril," Yahoo Sports, October 25, 2024. https://sports.yahoo.com/historic-house-ncaa-settlement-leaving-hundreds-of-olympic-sport-athletes-in-peril-125238713.html.
3. Dellenger. "Yahoo Is Part of the Yahoo Family of Brands."
4. X (Formerly Twitter). https://x.com/DarrenHeitner/status/1876984758921470062.

Index

Page numbers followed by *i* and *t* refer to illustrations and tables, respectively.

A

Addison, Christian, 28–30

Adidas, 158

Advance payments, 143, 147–149

Affiliates, 44–46

Africa, Josh, 110, 206

Agents, 171–189

   considerations before signing with, 173–177

   contracts with, 177–181

   need for, 108, 172–175

   parents, family members, and friends as, 186–188

   signing with the wrong agent, 182–186

   working with, 181–182

Algorithm-based content, 95

Allar, Drew, 64

Allbirds, 114

Alston awards, 6–7

Amazon affiliates, 45

Amazon Fanshop, 55

Ambassadors, 44–46

Antitrust law, 6, 8

Apparel, licensed, 33, 54, 117–118, 153, 158–160, 160*i. See also specific types of apparel*

Appearances, 52–54

Arby's, 119

Arenas, Elena, 161–162

Art, 69–72, 70*i*, 151

Athlete-focused marketplaces, 109–110

Attorneys, 140, 146, 149, 168, 173

Autographs, 52–54, 58, 152

B

Back pay provisions, 217–220

Bassitt, Trevor, 205–207, 210

Behind-the-scenes reels/posts, 103

Belibi, Fran, 95, 100

Bennett, Stetson, 52

Berry, Freddie, 120

Betts, Jack, 45–46, 113–114, 171–172

Big League Advance (BLA), 148

Big Ten Network, xvii

Bio, 92*i*, 92–94, 94*t*, 109

BLA (Big League Advance), 148

Blakeney, Coach (Howard University), 74

Blogs, 61

Bloom, Jeremy, 4–5

Board game, 56, 57*i*

Body Armor, 119

Books, 61–64, 62*i*, 151, 167–168

Boombah, 86

Boosters, 9–10, 13–14

Boost Mobile, 52–53

Booty, General, 45, 46, 56, 56*i*

Brady, Tom, 166

Brand-building content, 95–96

Brand-created content, 124

Brandr Group, 57, 155, 158, 163–165

Brands. *See also specific brands*
affiliates and ambassadors for, 44–46
basis of partnerships with, 85, 89, 95

co-branding, 152, 154–165
content created by, 124
contracts with, 192. *See also* Contracts
disclosing relationships with, 14, 43–44, 131
personal, *see* Personal brand
proactive outreach to, 112–123. *See also* Outreach to brands

Brand Squad, 146–147

BreakingT, 160

Breen, Sam, 86

Brennan, Myles, 72–73

Brown, Kane, 165

Brown, Reece, 74

BSN Sports, 207

Bueckers, Paige, 162, 167

Burks, Treylon, 85–86

BYU, 74–75

C

California Interscholastic Federation, 185–186

California NIL law, 7, 14

Camden, Anna, xvii, 47, 79, 212

Cameo, 68–69

Camps, 47–52

Campus Ink, 54, 55, 159, 160

Car deals, 72–73

Carter case, 217

Cash App, 110
Castro-Walker, Marcus,
    136–138
Cavinder, Haley, xvi, 40–41, 156
Cavinder, Hanna, xvi, 40–41, 156
Cavinder Twins brand, 40–41
CeraVe, 39
C4 Energy, 109
Champions (movie), 109
Champs, 39, 98
Channels, for social media
    marketing, 101
Charity, donating NIL money to,
    34, 64
Clapper, Leah, xvi–xvii, 56, 57*i*,
    79–80, 98, 102, 116,
    116*i*, 117
Clark, Dorie, 66–67
CLC (Collegiate Licensing
    Company), 4
Clemson University, 156
Clinics, 47–52
Coach, 113, 119
CoachTube, 49, 78
CoachUp, 49
Co-branding, 152, 154–155.
    See also Group licensing
Cole, Emily, 61–63, 62*i*,
    82–83, 92*i*, 92–93, 98,
    207–210, 213
Cole, Julia, 209
Coleman, Malachi, 64

Collectives, 133
    clarification of NCAA rules
        for, 9–10
    contracts with, 141–146
    deals through, 13–14,
        111–112
    models of, 133–134
    nonprofit, 134–135
    partnering with, 86
    school involvement with, 11
    variation in, 135–136
    working with, 133–146.
        *See also individual
        collectives*
Collegiate Licensing Company
    (CLC), 4
Colorado NIL law, 7, 14
Colors, as IP, 152, 153, 200
Commission, in agent contracts,
    178–180
Community building, 100–101
Compensation. *See also House v.
    NCAA;* Pricing
    in content creator contracts,
        194
    institutional rules for, 15–16
    for international athletes,
        21–22, 34
    NAIA rules for, 14
    NCAA institutional
        clarifications concerning,
        11–13

Compensation (*Continued*)
  NJCAA rules for, 15
  reductions in, 226
  written contract terms for,
    192–193
Content. *See also specific types of*
    content, e.g.: Posts
  algorithm-based, 95
  being strategic about, 94*i*,
    95–98. *See also* Social
    media marketing
  brand-building, 95–96
  brand-created, 124
  as intellectual property, 152
  ownership and usage rights
    of, 192
  and pricing of services, 126
  three-topic strategy for,
    83–84, 97
  user-generated, 129
  using intellectual property of
    others in, 152
Content creator contracts,
    193–202
  compensation and payment
    terms in, 194
  deliverables and expectations
    in, 198
  edits or modifications of
    content rights in, 199
  exclusivity agreements in,
    195–197

indemnification and liability
    in, 200
  for international students,
    34, 35
  licensing and usage rights in,
    194–195
  one-sided terms in or
    negotiations for, 201–202
  right of first refusal in,
    197–198
  termination clauses in,
    199–200
  use of school logos, colors, or
    facilities in, 200
Content creator pricing guide,
    127*t*–129*t*
Content franchises, 98–100
Contracts, 191–203
  attorneys for, 140, 146
  with collectives, 136–146
  for content creation, 193–202.
    See also Content creator
    contracts
  financial aid, 224
  future provisions in, *see*
    Future of NIL
  group-licensing, 156–157
  marketplaces' creation of, 111
  NCAA templates and
    guidance on, 131
  with NIL agents, 177–181
  written, benefits of, 192–193

Copyrights, 151, 152

Costs:

   of collectives, 134

   expense planning, for lessons, camps, or clinics, 51

   in pricing of services, 126

   of trademark filings, 166

Crain, Jake "JBoy," 61

Creator Institute, 62–63

Crimson Collective, 73

Crocs, 113

Cromartie, Marcus, 138

Crosby, Roscoe, 4

Cuban, Mark, 54

Cunningham, T.A., 185–186

Curran, Pat, xvii

CVS, 109, 113

D

Da La Haye, Donald, 4

Dancing with the Stars, 3–4

Daniels, JT, 161

Day in the Life as a D1 Volleyball Player, 208

Day in the Life of a Washed-Up D1 Volleyball Player, 208–209

Deals, 107–131. *See also* Monetizing NIL

   disclosure of, 14, 43–44, 131

   finding, 107–112

   for international students, 32–36

   negotiating, 123–130

   NJCAA stipulation concerning, 15

   pricing in, 124–130. *See also* Pricing

   proactive outreach to brands for, 112–123. *See also* Outreach to brands

   rules for, *see* NIL rules

   things to cover in, 123. *See also* Contracts

   through collectives, 111–112

   through marketplaces, 108–111

   through social media marketing, 89–90. *See also* Social media marketing

   and visas for international athletes, 27–28

Deliverables, in content creator contracts, 198

Designs, trademarks for, 152

Dexter, Gervon, 148

DGD Mafia, 58

Dick's Sporting Goods, 98

Disclosure of deals, 14, 43–44, 131

Disputes, with agents, 180–181

DMs:
  pitches via, 122–123
  reaching out to brands via, 114–115
  regularly checking, 112
Dončić, Luka, 168
Dosh, Kristi, 20
Dowling, Bailey, 55
Dunne, Olivia (Livvy), xvi, 41, 161

E
EA Sports video games, xv, 4, 162–163
Eastbay, 119
EB-1A (employment-based) visas, 25t–26t, 31–32
Edits to content, 126, 198, 199
Electronic Arts, 4
Email:
  pitch template for, 120–122
  reaching out to brands via, 115–120
  regularly checking, 112
Emergency preparation, for lessons, camps, or clinics, 50–51
Emmanuel, Hansel, 30
Empower program (Meta), xvii, 42, 99
Engagement:
  growing, 94–104

and number of followers, 84–85
Entrepreneurial You (Clark), 66
Envue Eye Center, 74
Equipment needs, for lessons, camps, or clinics, 50
Eskimo Joe's, 52
Etsy stores, 70
Everett Sports Marketing (ESM), 156
Exclusivity agreements, 194
  in content creator contracts, 195–197
  in contracts with collectives, 142–143
  with marketplaces, 111
  and pricing of services, 125
Exit 56, 63, 64
Expectations:
  in content creator contracts, 198
  in written contracts, 192
Expense planning, for lessons, camps, or clinics, 51
Expertise, in pricing of services, 125

F
F-1 (Academic Student) visas, 21–22, 23t, 27, 31–34
Facebook, *see individual users*

Facility arrangements, for lessons, camps, or clinics, 50

Fair Pay to Play Act (California), 7

Family members, as NIL agents, 186–188

Fanatics, 158, 161, 187–188

Farmer's Dog, 86

50 Cent, 154

Financial aid contracts, 224

Finnegan, Aleah, 161–162

First refusal rights, 197–198

502 Circle, 135

FlightPath, 110

Florida NIL law, 7, 14, 39, 148

Florida State, 138

Florida Victorious, 134, 135

Fly Like Chi! (Coleman), 64

Following:
    for finding brand partners, 107–108
    growing your, 94–104

Ford, 40

Fouts, Montana, 54, 68, 86

Frazier, Caroline, 79, 83–84

Free products and services, 72–76

Friends, as NIL agents, 186–188

Friends and teammates reels/posts, 104

Frieser, Joshua, 178, 179

Frix, Ty, 58

FTC requirements, for monetizing NIL, 43–44

Funny reels/posts, 102–103

Future of NIL, 215–229
    compensation reductions and termination, 226
    morality clauses, 226–227
    ongoing legal challenges, 228
    revenue sharing, 216–226.
        See also Revenue sharing
    roster and scholarship changes, 221–224
    transfer portal restrictions, 225
    waiver clauses, 227–228

G

Gallegos, Marquis, 139–140

Galloway, Brevin, 208

Gary Yamamoto Custom Baits, 86

Gator Collective, 16, 54, 134, 137

Georgia High School Association, 17, 185

Georgia NIL law, 14, 216

Gerben, Josh, 155, 165–167

Getty Images, 154

Gillette, 109

Glover, Alex, 206–209, 212

G.O.A.T. Fuel, 119

Gobourne, Derrian, 182–184

Gobourne, Tikisha, 182–184, 186

Godin, Seth, 81

253

Index

Gordon McKernan Injury
Attorneys, 69
Green, Patton, 21
Green, Sam, 66, 95–96, 100, 101,
206, 209–212
Green cards, 25*t*, 31, 32
GreenPrint Real Estate
Group, 61
Griffin, Chase, 53, 171
Group licensing, 57–58, 154–165
creative opportunities for,
163–165
jerseys and shirzees, 158
opting into agreements for,
155–157
trading cards, 161–162
T-shirts and other apparel,
159–160, 160*i*
video games, 162–163
Group of 5 schools, 2, 220

H
Hadid, Gigi, 154
Hagens Berman, 218-219
Hally Shade Stix, 165
Halter, Emma, 68–69
Hamilton, Leonard, 138
Harris, Spencer, 139, 140
Harrison, Marvin, Jr., 187–188
Harrison, Marvin, Sr., 187
Hasan, Mo, 59, 212–213
Hashtags, 96

Hathcock, Hugh, 137–138
Hayes, Ryan, 63–64
Heitner, Darren, 141–142,
156, 173, 175–176,
191, 226
Hennessy, Brittany, 126–130
HEYDUDE, 109
Higgins, Laney, 39, 41–43, 42*i*,
54, 55*i*, 95, 97–99,
117–118, 211–212
High school athletes:
Mississippi NIL law for, 7
NIL rights for, xv
NIL rules for, 3, 17–18
use of school IP in deals by,
153
Hollingsworth Richards Ford,
72–73
HomeGrown, 70
Hoosiers Connect, 135
Hoosiers for Good, 135
Hop Topic, 109
House, Grant, 216–217
House of Victory, 139–140
House v. NCAA, 7, 14, 135,
139–140, 146,
216–225
Howard University, 73–74
H&R Block, 98, 110
Hubbard case, 217
Hunter, Travis, 86
Hustle & Harmony, 209

I

ICON collective, 54
Idlette, Shani, 110
iHeart Radio, 59
Illinois NIL law, 7
Indemnification, in content
    creator contracts, 200
Indiana University, 135
INFLCR, 89, 109
Influencer (Hennessy), 126
Influencer marketplaces, 110
Instagram, 18. *See also specific
    users*
  building communities on,
    100–101
  compensation for posts on, 40
  content creator pricing guide
    for, 127*t*–128*t*
  getting verified on,
    104–106
  hashtags on, 96
  monetizing, 78
  popularity of, 101
  reaching out to brands
    via, 114
Institutional rules, 3, 15–17
  changes in, 215–216
  NCAA institutional
    involvement
    clarifications, 10–13
Insurance, for lessons, camps, or
    clinics, 49

Intellectual property (IP):
  licensing, *see* Licensing
    intellectual property
  of others, 152–154
Intercollegiate athletics,
    organizations
    governing, 2. *See also*
    College athletes
International student-athletes:
  limitations on NIL for,
    32–36
  NIL risks for, 35–36
  NIL rules for, 21–36
  resources and news for, 37
  trademarks for, 165
  types of visas for,
    22–31, 23*t*–26*t*. *See also*
    Visas for international
    student-athletes
Invesco QQQ, 114
IP, *see* Intellectual property
Irrevocability, of
    contracts, 194

J

Jacksons Food Stores, 161
James, LeBron, 166
The JBoy Show, 60–61
Jefferson, Richard, xvii
Jerseys, 57, 58, 154, 158
Johnson, Flau'jae, 69
Johnson, Meechie, 208

K

Kardashian, Khloe, 154
KastKing, 86
Kay Jewelers, 3
Kazadi, Ra-Sun, 70–72
Keegan, Amanda, 64
Keegan, Trevor, 63–64
Kelce, Jason, 166
Kelce, Travis, 166
Keller, Sam, 4, 5, 75
Keller Williams, 74
Knox, Trey, 83, 86
Kuzmeski, Maribeth, 146–147

L

Lawrence, Blake, 85
Leaf, 161–162
Learfield/Collegiate Licensing
    Company, 158
Lechner, Hannah, 18–21,
    122–123
Lechner, Reese, 18–21, 122–123
Lessons, providing, 47–52
Liability, in content creator
    contracts, 200
Liability waivers, for lessons,
    camps, or clinics, 50
Licensing intellectual property,
    151–169
    co-branding, 154–165
    content creator contract rights
        for, 194–195

group licensing, 154–165.
    See also Group licensing
for international students, 34
and IP belonging to others,
    152–154
NIL Store licenses, 55
photos, 130
trademarks, 165–168
Lifestyle reels/posts, 103–104
LifeWallet, 138
Likeness of college athletes, in
    EA Sports video games,
    xv. *See also* Name,
    image, and likeness
    (NIL)
Like To Know It (LTK), 45, 78
Limited liability companies
    (LLCs), 49, 79
LinkedIn, 101, 115
Links:
    in getting verified on
        Instagram, 104–105
    and pricing of services, 126
    in social media marketing,
        90, 93, 94*t*
Liquid IV, 109
LLCs (limited liability
    companies), 49, 79
Logos, 152, 165, 200
Lopez, Jennifer, 154
Los Angeles Daily News, 139–140
Louisiana State University, 153

LTK (Like To Know It), 45, 78
Ludwig, Marty, 158
Lululemon, 39, 42, 99, 117–118, 211–212
Lynch, Keshawn, 109

M
McKinney, Syd, 69–70, 70*i*, 78, 212
Maiorova, Ksenia, 22, 27–28, 31–36
Maldonado, Amy, 27–28, 32–36
Manning, Arch, 163
Manning, Peyton, 166
Marketing agencies, 146–147
Marketing plan:
  for lessons, camps, or clinics, 50
  for social media, *see* Social media marketing
Marketplaces, finding deals through, 108–111
Marks, Daniel, 73–74
Marshall, Keith, 58
Massachusetts Collective, 86
Mayfield, Baker, 188
M Den, 158
Medical services, 73–74
Memorabilia, 54–57, 55*i*–57*i*
Memorandums of Understanding (MOUs), 225–227

The Men in Back (Allar), 64
The Men Up Front (Tengwall), 64
The Men Up Front (Zinter, Keegan, and Hayes), 63–64
Merchandise, 54–57, 55*i*–57*i*
Mercury podcast network, 60
Meta Empower program, xvii, 42, 99
Meta Verified, 104–106
Micro-influencers, 84, 89
Migos, 109
Military service academies, 17
Mission Waco, 48
Mississippi NIL law, 7
Mitchell, Chloe, 1, 40, 60, 130
Modification of content, 199
MOGL, 109
Momentum Podcast, 59, 213
Monetizing NIL, 1, 39–76.
  See also Deals; Pricing
  active and passive income generation, 32–36
  affiliate and ambassador roles, 44–46
  appearances and autographs, 52–54
  art, 69–72, 70*i*
  books, 61–64, 62*i*
  car deals, 72–73
  first allowances of, 1–2

257

Index

Monetizing NIL (*Continued*)
  free products and services,
    72–76
  FTC requirements for,
    43–44
  future of, 215–216. *See also*
    Future of NIL
  group licensing and
    team-wide deals, 57–58
  lessons, camps, and clinics,
    47–52
  medical services, 73–74
  merchandise and
    memorabilia, 54–57,
    55*i*–57*i*
  music, 69
  non-fungible tokens, 58
  podcasts, radio, and blogs,
    58–61
  public speaking and
    messaging, 65–69
  real estate training, 74–75
  social media marketing,
    40–44, 41*i*, 42*i*
Morality clauses, 226–227
Motivational reels/posts, 102
MOUs (Memorandums of
    Understanding),
    225–227
Mulvaney, Ryan, 225–227
Murray, Aaron, 58
Music, 69, 151

N
NAIA (National Association
    of Intercollegiate
    Athletics), 2
NAIA NIL rules, xv, 3, 14
Name, image, and likeness
    (NIL). *See also* Personal
    brand; *specific topics,
    e.g.:* Agents
  defined, 1
  developing strategy for,
    77–84, 81*i*
  future of, *see* Future of NIL
  as intellectual property, 151
  keys to success with, 120
  monetizing, 1. *See also*
    Monetizing NIL
  myths about, 39–40
  rights to, xv, 6
Names, trademarks for, 152, 165
Nano-influencers, 84, 89
Napier, Billy, 136–138
Napier, Shabazz, 6
National Association of
    Intercollegiate Athletics
    (NAIA), xv, 2, 3, 14
National Collegiate Athletic
    Association (NCAA), 2,
    193, 215
  House v. NCAA, 7, 14, 135,
    139–140, 146, 216–225
  NCAA v. Alston, 217–218

NIL rules of, 3–14. *See also* NCAA NIL rules

Transfer Portal, 225

National Junior College Athletic Association (NJCAA), xiv, 2, 15

National Letter of Intent system, 224

National X Immigration (Maiorova and Maldonado), 27, 31

NCAA, *see* National Collegiate Athletic Association

NCAA NIL rules, xv, 3–14

early application of, 40–41

evolution of, 9–14

frequently asked questions about, 8–9

legal challenges to, 4–8. *See also specific cases*

for money received from collectives, 135–136

on pay-for-play deals, 144

prior to 2021, 3

waivers to, 3–4

NCAA v. Alston, 6, 8, 217–218

Nebraska NIL law, 14

Negotiation. *See also* Contracts

of content creator contracts, 201–202

of deals, 123–130

The Next Round, 61

NFTs (non-fungible tokens), 58, 161

Niches, brand, 84–86

Nicknames:

as intellectual property, 151

for social media, 90–91

trademarks for, 165, 167

Nike, 3, 158, 197

NIL, *see* Name, image, and likeness

NIL entities, school involvement with, 11

NIL FanBox, 163–164, 164*i*

NILIsland.com, 102

Nilly, 148–149

NIL Real Estate, 74–75

NIL rules, 1–38

changes to, xv–xvi, 1–3

for high school athletes, 17–18

history of, 3–8

institutional rules, 15–17

for international student-athletes, 21–37

NAIA, xv, 3, 14

NCAA, 3–14. *See also* NCAA NIL rules

NJCAA, xv, 15

for youth athletes, 18–21

NIL Store, 54, 55, 55*i*

98Strong, 109

Nix, Bo, 61
NJCAA (National Junior College Athletic Association), 2
NJCAA NIL rules, xv, 15
Non-fungible tokens (NFTs), 58, 161
Nonprofit collectives, 134–135
Notre Dame, 220

O
O-1/O-1A (Individuals with Extraordinary Ability or Achievement) visas, 22, 24*t*, 27, 30
O'Bannon, Ed, xv, 5–6
Odum, Shy, 74
Ogunbowale, Arike, 3–4
Ohio NIL law, 216
Ohio State University, 153
Oklahoma State University, 146–147
Oliver, Tamir, 216–217
Omaha Steaks, 114
OneTeam Partners, 57, 155, 156, 158, 160, 161
ONIT, 162
Opendorse, 85, 89, 109, 111
Osborne, Tom, 64
Outback, 39
Outreach to brands, 112–123
    how and who in, 114–116

pitches for, 116*i,* 116–123. *See also* Pitches
Ownership rights, in written contracts, 192

P
P-1A (Athlete) visas, 23*t*–24*t,* 27–30
Panini, 3, 161, 162
Panini College, 162
Parents, as NIL agents, 186–188
Park Avenue, 156
Passive income-generating activities, 32–36, 46
Pavia, Diego, 160
Pay-for-play deals, 9, 144
Payment terms. *See also* Compensation
    back pay provisions, 217–220
    in content creator contracts, 194
    in written contracts, 194
Pearpop, 165
Pedialyte, 113
Pehlke, Mitchell, 98
Percentage of deals, contract terms for, 144–145
Performance Center, 18–19
Perkins, Kendrick, 148–149
Perpetuity clauses, 142–144, 194

Personal brand. *See also* Name, image, and likeness (NIL); *specific people*
  beyond college, 79–80. *See also* Post-college personal brand
  defining and growing your, 77–86
  developing strategy for, 77–84, 81*i*
  fluctuation in, 82
  as intellectual property, 152
  for international athletes, 37
  niches for, 84–86
  three bucket exercise for, 80–84, 81*i*
  words and marks defining, 168
Personality, 166
PetSmart, 83, 86
Photos:
  copyright protection of, 151
  as intellectual property, 151
  for NIL marketplaces, 109
  school IP policies for, 153
  selling rights to, 129–130
  social media, 90, 91, 93*t,* 96
  taken by others, 154
Phrases, trademarks for, 167
Pitches, 116*i,* 116–123
  by DM, 122–123
  email template for, 120–122

examples of, 117–120
  key points in, 116, 116*i*
  mistakes made in, 117
PlayBooked, 110
Players' Lounge, 58
The Player's Plate (Cole), 61–63, 62*i,* 207, 209
Poa, Last-Tear, 30
Podcasts, 58–61
Poncius, Hunter, 159
Post-college personal brand, 79–80, 205–214
  making connections for, 212–213
  and working with brands, 206–212
Postgame, 109
Posts:
  adding location to, 96
  ideas for, 102–104
  as intellectual property, 152
  by social media mangers for international athletes, 34–35
  in social media marketing, 89. *See also* Social media marketing
  three-topic strategy for, 83–84
Power 4 schools, 2
Power 5 schools, 2, 135, 216–220

Pricing, 124–130
  elements of, 125–126
  formula for, 126–127,
    127t–129t
  for lessons, camps, or
    clinics, 51
  for speaking, 66–68
Prince, Sedona, 216–217
Printful, 56
Profile, for NIL marketplaces,
  109
Profile, social media:
  bio for, 92i, 92–94, 94t
  links in, 90, 93, 94t
  optimizing, 90
  photo for, 91, 93t
  username for, 90–91, 93, 93t
Publicity rights, see Licensing
  intellectual property
Public speaking and messaging,
  65–69

Q
Q-Collar, 99
Q30 Innovations, 39
Quest Nutrition, 39

R
Radio shows, 60–61
Raising Cane's, 52
Ramos, Matt, 159
Rashada, Jaden, 136–138

Raymond, Michael, 82, 83,
    172–173, 176, 181–184,
    207–208
Raymond Representation, 82
Real estate training, 74–75
Reels, ideas for, 102–104
Revenue sharing, 216–226,
    See also *House v. NCAA*
  back pay provisions,
    217–220
  compensation reductions and
    termination, 226
  model for, 220–221
  NCAA NIL rules clarification
    for, 11–12
  new agreements for,
    224–225
  roster and scholarship
    changes for, 221–224
  transfer portal restrictions, 225
Ricciardi, Chris, 149
Richardson, Anthony, 168
Richardson, Demani, 61
Right of first refusal, in content
    creator contracts,
    197–198
Rivers, Bruce, 73–74
Roberson, Aaron, 74
Roberts, Nora, 113
Robins, Calvin, Jr., 74
Rock 'Em Socks, 45
Rogers, Camryn, 31

262

Index

Roster changes, 221–224
Royalties, 57, 89, 158–160, 162
Ruiz, John, 137–138

S
Sanchez-Vicario, Arantxa, 188
Sanders, Spencer, 52
Schoenherr, Savannah, 161–162
Scholarship changes, 6, 221–224
School logos, colors, or facilities, 200
Scope of representation, in agent contracts, 179
Second Spoon, 212
Shirzees (T-shirt jerseys), 57, 58, 154, 158
Shough, Tyler, 86
Signature, as intellectual property, 151
Simmons, Riley, 65–66, 210–211
Simpson, Jessica, 154
Slogans, trademarks for, 165, 167
Sluka, Matthew, 138
Smart Cups, 113
SMILE surgery, 73–74
Smith, Rayquan, 113, 119–120
Snapchat, 40
Social media, reaching out to brands via, 114–115. *See also specific platforms*

Social media marketing, 40–44, 41*i*, 42*i*, 89–106. *See also specific types of media and platforms*
bio for, 90, 92*i*, 92–94, 94*t*
building community in, 100–101
channels for, 101
content franchises for, 98–100
FTC requirements for, 43–44
growing following and engagement in, 94–104
Instagram verification for, 104–106
links in, 90, 93, 94*t*
niches in, 84–86
optimizing profile in, 90
posting ideas for athletes in, 102–104
pricing guide for content creators, 127*t*–129*t*
profile photo for, 90, 91, 93*t*
social content strategy, 94*i*, 95–98
username for, 90–91, 93, 93*t*
Software, copyright protection of, 151
Sole discretion, 198
Sony Music, 165
Spiller, Isaiah, 61
SportsBizMiss, 91
Sprayground, 114

Staff, for lessons, camps, or clinics, 51
State high school sports associations, 3, 17–18, 39, 153
State laws, 3, 7. *See also individual states*
  for agent registration, 175
  continuing evolution of, 14
  for contracts with players under 18, 191–192
Stitching content, xvii
Stokols, Steven, *see individual users*
Student-Athlete.co, 48, 49
Summit Stands, 86
Sunday Golf, 21
Super Glow, 161
SURGE program, 207
Swift, Taylor, 166
Symbols, trademarks for, 152

T
Tarango, Tracy, 30
Target, 40
Taxes:
  on car deals, 73
  with collectives, 134, 135
  on free products, services, leases, and travel, 75
Team-wide deals, 57–58. *See also* Group licensing

Tengwall, Landon, 64
Term, of agent contracts, 177–178
Termination clauses, 226
  in agent contracts, 179–180
  in content creator contracts, 199–200
TexAgs.com, 61, 161
Texas A&M, 12
Texas NIL law, 7
Therabody, 98
Third parties, 133–150. *See also specific parties*
  collectives, 111–112, 133–146. *See also* Collectives
  deals with, 13–14
  for group licensing deals, 57
  licensing companies, 158
  marketing agencies, 146–147
  permission for schools' IP use with, 153
  that offer advances, 147–149
Three bucket exercise, 80–84, 81*i*, 97
TikTok, 18. *See also specific users*
  compensation for posts on, 40
  content creator pricing guide for, 128*t*
  popularity of, 101
Timme, Drew, 52
Title IX rules, 221

264
Index

Topps, 161
Top Tier Authentics, 55
Trademarks, 151, 152, 165–168
Trading cards, 53, 57, 58, 154, 161–162
Trahan, Ryan, 4
Transfer portal restrictions, 158, 225
Transformational reels/posts, 102
Tshiebwe, Oscar, 35
T-shirts, 52–54, 56*i,* 152, 154, 159–160, 160*i*
Twitter (now X), 40, 90, 101
Two Circles, 156

U
Ulmer, Will "Lucky Bill," 69, 78
Under Armour, 158
U.S. Citizenship and Immigration Services (USCIS), 30
University of Florida, 15–16, 134, 136–138
University of Louisville, 135
University of Michigan, 158
University of Nevada, Las Vegas (UNLV), 138
University of North Carolina, 152
University of Oklahoma, 153
University of South Carolina, 156
University of Southern California (USC), 139–140, 153

University of Texas, 152
University of Utah, 73
UNLV, 138
Upper Deck, 161
Urbani, Cate, 47–48
Usage rights, in contracts, 192, 194–195
USC, 139–140, 153
USCIS (U.S. Citizenship and Immigration Services), 30
User-generated content, 129
Username, for social media marketing, 90–91, 93, 93*t*
Ustby, Alyssa, 208

V
Valby, Parker, 197
Van Wyk, Kieron, 28, 29
Video games, 154, 162–163
  EA Sports, xv, 4, 162–163
  group licensing for, 57
  lawsuits over, 4
Videos, 96, 152
Violations of NCAA interim policy, 12
Virginia NIL law, 14, 216
Virtual speaking deals, 68
Visas for international student-athletes, 21
  EB-1A, 25*t*–26*t,* 31–32
  F-1, 21–22, 23*t,* 27, 31–34
  O-1/O-1A, 22, 24*t,* 27, 30

Visas for international student-athletes (*Continued*)
outdated regulations for, 22
P-1A, 22, 23*t*–24*t*, 27–30
qualifying for, 27
reviews of, 37
types of, 22–27, 23*t*–26*t*
Vodopia, Andy, 63–64
Voice, as intellectual property, 151
Volunteers, for lessons, camps, or clinics, 51

W
W4LKING and T4LKING series, 41–42, 99, 117–118, 211
Wagbnb, 86
Waiver clauses, 227–228
Walmart, 40
Warfield, Isiah, 74
WaterLand Co, 86
Wathen, Becca, 97, 99, 105, 106

Wells, Antwane, Jr., 86
Wilcoxson, Cody, 145, 179, 183
Wilken, Claudia, 6

X
X (formerly Twitter), 40, 90, 101

Y
YMCA, 47
Youth athletes:
NIL rights for, xv
NIL rules for, 18–21
YouTube, 18. *See also specific users*
compensation for posts on, 40
content creator pricing guide for, 129*t*

Z
Zinter, Zak, 63–64
ZipRecruiter, 110